PRAYER BOOK

BOOK

FOR LAY PEOPLE

Common Worship Services
with Introductions by Canon Stephen Lake,
Subdean of St Albans Cathedral

First published in Great Britain in 2008

Society for Promoting Christian Knowledge
36 Causton Street
London SW1P 4ST

British Library Cataloguing-in-Publication Data
A catalogue record for this book is available from the British Library

ISBN 978–0–281–06038–2

1 3 5 7 9 10 8 6 4 2

Designed and typeset by Kenneth Burnley, Wirral, Cheshire
Printed in Great Britain by Cromwell Press

Produced on paper from sustainable forests

CONTENTS

Using this Book   iv

Introduction   1

The Eucharist   7
    The *Common Worship* Service   21

Holy Communion at Home or in Hospital   63
    The *Common Worship* Service   67

The Church's Year   71
    The *Common Worship* Calendar   83

Holy Days   87
    Common Worship: Holy Days   91

Readings for the Main Service on Sundays and Festivals   101
    The *Common Worship* Readings   105

The Reconciliation of a Penitent   115
    The *Common Worship* Service   119

Holy Baptism within a Celebration of Holy Communion   125
    The *Common Worship* Service   131

Confirmation outside the Order for Celebration of
    Holy Communion   147
    The *Common Worship* Service   151

The Marriage Service   161
    The *Common Worship* Service   165

The Funeral Service   177
    The *Common Worship* Service   181

An Order for Night Prayer (Compline)   197
    The *Common Worship* Service   199

Psalms for Sundays and Festivals   207
    The *Common Worship* Psalms   209

Prayers for Daily Life and Occasions at Home   299

USING THIS BOOK

There are two kinds of material in this book: *Common Worship* services, and (with a line down the left-hand side) material to help in the understanding of the purpose and shape of each service. As part of its worship material, the book includes the psalms used on Sundays and festivals, some collects and a few prayers for use at home.

In *Common Worship* there are many possible variations and alternative prayers that may be used, as well as resources of extra and seasonal material. This is all available on the internet (search for *Common Worship* texts, and then enter the aspect that you are interested in) and in five larger *Common Worship* books (Church House Publishing).

In setting out the services in this book some rubrics and texts, which are intended for the clergy and those leading services, have been omitted.

INTRODUCTION

God is spirit, and those who worship him must
worship in spirit and truth. (John 4.24)

Worship is giving God his 'worth'. In prayer together we
engage with God the Father who has engaged with us,
uniquely in the incarnation of his Son, Jesus Christ.
Through the power of the Holy Spirit we continue this
dynamic relationship and our worship is an offering to
God of everything we are and everything we praise him
for being. Worship is the natural response of every Christian to the love of God in Christ. Worship can take many
forms and be glorious (and not so glorious) but if we offer
our worship to God with sincerity and with open hearts
to his will, we will be worshipping in spirit and truth.

The Church has the task of worshipping. The Church
is a worshipping community, so it provides resources for
public and private worship. In the Church of England, this
material is to be found in the Book of Common Prayer
and in *Common Worship*. To support *Common Worship*,
Prayer Book for Lay People provides an overview of the
most commonly used services from *Common Worship*
and offers help with understanding worship and making
the most of these special moments. Make this book your

friend and feel free to use it in church, at home and everywhere.

LITURGY AND WORSHIP

Worship is the general term for all Christian praise. The word 'liturgy' comes from the Greek word *leitourgia* and essentially means public worship. 'The liturgy' also refers to the textual parts of a service and the way in which the service is presented. So if 'worship' is what we are doing, liturgy is what we are using and how we are doing the worship. The terms are often interchangeable. Liturgical worship has a number of characteristics. It is:

- *Public* – worship is not simply a private enterprise, it is also a proclamation of what the Church believes in common.
- *Corporate* – we worship together, whether as a number of people in one place at one time, or as the body of Christ in all places at all times.
- *Relational* – the liturgy connects us with others worshipping in similar ways in other parts of the world and down the ages.
- *Real* – recognizing that a moment of worship has significance for the whole of our lives and the way we live.
- *Recognizable* – the liturgy is not just words; it is action too with movement, participation, drama, symbol and music.
- *Formational* – worship changes us; it challenges our preconceptions and forms us as Christians in the world.

COMMON WORSHIP

Anglican worship has a broad range and rich variety. However, there are identifiable characteristics that are held in common and these show who we are and what we believe.

Common Worship was introduced in 2000 after an extensive process of creation, scrutiny and authorization. Building on the tradition of the Book of Common Prayer (1662) and the changing worship over the centuries, *Common Worship* provides a family of texts and resources that can be used in a wide range of circumstances. The liturgy is used by a vast number of communities in many different situations. If it is to be both fulfilling and 'fit for purpose' it is therefore important that it should have variety. But it is also important that our worship be structured and recognizable as belonging to the An-glican tradition. *Common Worship* enables a sense of unity without uniformity and helps us avoid the excesses of personal taste and the dangers of ignorance. This is espe-cially important for Anglicans, as our doctrine – what we actually believe about God – is to be found in our worship and the historic formularies of the Church.

Anglican worship, as expressed in *Common Worship*, is grounded in the Bible, has a recognizable structure and a common lectionary (a table of readings for set days; see p. 101). It has central texts and a sense of connection with the whole Christian tradition. In other words, Anglican worship is not solely congregational; that is, it is not determined solely by the local community for its own use. Our liturgy is bigger than that: it is rooted in local expression and lived out in daily lives, but it also belongs to us all and therefore should be accessible to all, having a 'catholic' or universal perspective. The Anglican vision is rooted in Scripture, Tradition and Reason and this vision is best expressed through our recognizable worship of God.

Common Worship is based around these commonalities but has a wide range of resources for the needs of today's Church. The full range of *Common Worship* resources is widely available but many worshippers will only be familiar with the core Sunday book or specially produced local orders of service. In the rarely read preface to the core Sunday book, the ethos for *Common Worship* is described. It says:

Worship not only strengthens Christians for witness and service, but is itself a forum in which Christ is made known. Worship is for the whole people of God, who are fellow pilgrims on a journey of faith, and those who attend services are all at different stages of that journey. Indeed, worship itself is a pilgrimage – a journey into the heart of the love of God. A number of the services themselves – particularly that of Holy Baptism – are celebrated in stages. In each case the journey through the liturgy has a clear structure with signposts for those less familiar with the way. It moves from the gathering of the community through the Liturgy of the Word to an opportunity of transformation, sacramental or non-sacramental, after which those present are sent out to put their faith into practice ...

It is when the framework of worship is clear and familiar and the texts are known by heart that the poetry of praise and the passion of prayer can transcend the printed word. Then worship can take wing and become the living sacrifice of ourselves to the God whose majesty is beyond compare and whose truth is from everlasting.

STRUCTURE, SHAPE AND SPIRIT

Prayer Book for Lay People provides the essential texts for regular worship and a pastoral and liturgical introduction to each section. These introductions aim to help the worshipper – you – to find your way around the *Common Worship* texts and to have these readily to hand.

Each introduction follows a similar pattern.

STRUCTURE
- What is in the service?
- How is the service laid out?
- What are the key elements of this liturgy?

SHAPE
- What is this act of worship saying?
- What are the practical aspects that we will see and recognize?
- How is this liturgy presented?

- What does this liturgy mean?
- How are you to be transformed by this time in worship?
- How can you prepare to receive the most from God through this worship?

SPIRIT AND TRUTH

Worship is not a science or an examination to be passed. It is an engagement with the living God. *Common Worship* is not the last word in liturgy but it is the pattern of worship in the Church of England that articulates today our corporate and current response to God's love in Christ. May we all ever deepen in our love of Christ and thrive as we enjoy the worship of his Church.

THE EUCHARIST

The Eucharist is at the very heart of all Christian worship and therefore of *Common Worship*. Instituted by Christ himself (see 1 Corinthians 11.23–26), the Eucharist is *the* central act for Christians when they come together in worship. In the Eucharist we encounter Christ in the Word and uniquely in the form of bread and wine, the body and blood of Jesus. From the earliest times, Christians have come together to share in the 'breaking of the bread' and the prayers. St Paul records the earliest written account of the Eucharist in 1 Corinthians, and the Gospels each have their own record of the Last Supper. So ever since that first Maundy Thursday in Jerusalem, for the Church big and small, in secret and in the open air, with great drama and as a simple sharing among friends, the Eucharist has been the main act of worship that has brought Christians together to acknowledge the living presence of Christ in our lives. The Eucharist as one of the sacraments shows us that God meets us through outward and visible signs that have inward and spiritual grace.

The Eucharist has several titles, each expressing a certain emphasis. In *Common Worship* the titles given are 'Holy Communion': giving a sense of our communion with God through receiving the bread and the wine; the 'Eucharist': from the Greek word meaning thanksgiving, meaning that we give thanks as Christ did; and the 'Lord's Supper': recalling the direct link with Christ's last meal with his disciples. All these and other titles for this service are valid and some titles have become code for expressing the way in which this service may be presented. So a service of Holy Communion is often a said, short service, perhaps the first service on a Sunday morning, while a Parish Eucharist will be the main celebration on a Sunday morning with hymns, sermon and a real sense of the worshipping community coming together. *Common Worship* provides a wealth of different forms of the Eucharist, in modern language and traditional language, all with a rich supply of options and resources to make every service appropriate for individual need and seasonal focus.

STRUCTURE

The Eucharist naturally falls into two main parts: the Liturgy of the Word and the Liturgy of the Sacrament. The Liturgy of the Word begins at the first reading, and contains Old and New Testament readings, a psalm, the Gospel reading, the Sermon (when the scriptural word is reflected upon and proclaimed), the Creed and the Prayers of Intercession. This first half of the liturgy will be focused on the lectern and pulpit. The Liturgy of the Sacrament begins with the Peace and continues until almost the end of the service. It contains the Preparation of the Table, the Taking of the Bread and Wine, the Eucharistic Prayer, the Lord's Prayer, the Breaking of the Bread, the Giving of Communion and the Prayer after Communion. This second 'half' of the liturgy will be focused on the holy table or altar. This duality shows the importance of both key elements – the Word of God through Scripture and the action of God through his sacramental gifts.

Common Worship provides for the Eucharist, and subsequently for several other services, an outline structure, which shows the nature of the liturgy. The structure of the Eucharist follows this pattern:

The people and the priest greet each other in the Lord's name

It is made clear from the outset that the Eucharist is not just a priestly activity with the people as spectators. Priest and people celebrate together. While some may have specific roles, it is in the coming together around the altar to hear the Word broken open and then to share the bread and wine that creates the eucharistic community. *Common Worship* therefore emphasizes this by giving this opening section of the liturgy up to the Liturgy of the Word the title of 'The Gathering'.

This is given form by the familiar words of Christian greeting:

> The Lord be with you
> **and also with you**.

In some churches this is preceded by an invocation of the Trinity. The priest taking the service is referred to as the president. This is because the president presides over the whole service, drawing together the community into worship, using key points to lead the people: this opening greeting, the Absolution, the Collect, the Peace, the Eucharistic Prayer and the Blessing. Some parishes like the name 'celebrant' for the priest leading the service. But in *Common Worship*, all the people are 'celebrating' the Eucharist. Some parishes may enjoy the ministry of a deacon, an assistant priest or a lay reader, and this servant ministry can be expressed by the deacon (or other minister) reading the Gospel, preparing the table and gifts and dismissing the people.

The people and the priest confess their sins and are assured of God's forgiveness

Saying sorry is something we often do, but rarely mean. In the Eucharist we should always mean what we say, and act upon it, for that is what God does for us. The Prayers of Penitence often begin with seasonal introductions and then lead the gathered community into a corporate confession. We gather all our shortcomings, failures and deliberately negative actions into one general expression of sorrow. God's response is immediate and fulsome – forgiveness. Restoration is given and we are free to begin again, so naturally the response is to sing the song of the angels and to proclaim, 'Glory to God in the highest'. (For a more detailed consideration of reconciliation see the later section on page 115.)

The people and the priest keep silence and pray a Collect

Silence is an important part of worship. It should not be false or contrived but full of meaning and personal reflection. Having made confession and been forgiven, we keep silence for a moment to offer our own thoughts and prayers before the president gathers (collects) the themes of the day into a common expression of praise, thanksgiving and supplication.

The people and the priest proclaim and respond to the word of God

The Liturgy of the Word begins and the worshipping community move into a receiving mode as the Word is proclaimed and taught. The controlling factor is the Gospel of the day and a preacher will always make this the starting point. According to the lectionary, the readings are given and the sermon unpacks their meaning with relevance for the prevailing real-life situation. Our corporate response to this reading and interpretation of Scripture is to gather our common faith into the words of the Creed. The Creed or another form of authorized affirmation of faith should always be used on Sundays and special days. Through this general recitation we show our membership of the body of Christ and acknowledge our interdependence with God and each other.

The people and the priest pray for the Church and the world

A lay person often leads the intercessions. The task here is to pray on behalf of the people, not to give a second sermon. While this is a place for greater flexibility and individual expression, there is an agreed formula for good intercession for and on behalf of others. We pray for:

- the Church of Christ;
- creation, human society, the Sovereign and those in authority;
- the local community;
- those who suffer;
- the communion of saints;
- those who have died.

Feel free to offer names for prayer in any church that you are attending for worship.

The people and the priest exchange the Peace

The Liturgy of the Sacrament begins as we start to become less objective and more intimate. Standing together, and often with a demonstrative action, we take the opportunity to be literally at peace with one another before God makes his peace with us. Different practices and enthusiasms for the Peace exist in all our parishes.

The people and the priest prepare the table

During the singing of a hymn, the offertory is made, the giving of bread and wine from among the gifts of God. As well as these gifts of creation we offer our money and indeed our whole selves for God to do what we cannot do ourselves.

The people and the priest pray the Eucharistic Prayer

During the Eucharistic Prayer, the liturgy comes to a crescendo. This summary denotes what is going on in this vital moment:

> Gathered around the altar table, with bread and wine as their focus, the president and people now pray the eucharistic prayer, a sustained outpouring of praise, that identifies with Jesus in the second of the four actions at the supper [described on page 17], but develops beyond this into thanksgiving for the mighty acts of God in Christ himself, recalls the supper and the words during it, calls down the Holy Spirit in relation to the gifts and the people, and offers the duty and service of Christian hearts.
> Michael Perham
> *New Handbook of Pastoral Liturgy*

Eucharistic Prayers are said by priests for us. But make this special moment your own. Be sure to listen to the words, and to have read and reflected upon the printed Eucharistic Prayers for they seek to meet people where they are, and so work on many different levels. There are eight Eucharistic Prayers to choose from, each containing a different emphasis. Especially during the seasonal times, the Prefaces tell of the wonderful mighty acts of God. The Lord's Prayer (in either modern or traditional language) is used at this point.

The people and the priest break the bread

The bread is broken as a practical necessity in order to be shared with the people. This has particular power when there is one bread, one loaf. Yet deeper than that, the bread is broken to symbolize the breaking of Christ's body on the cross, so that the gift of his sacrifice can be shared by all. 'Though we are many, we are one body, because we all share in one bread.' (See also the comments on the Eucharist on p. 17.)

The people and the priest receive communion

The president now invites the people to communion. Local practice will determine exactly how this is administered, but there should always be an atmosphere of reverence and reflection followed by a time of thanksgiving. A choir may sing or hymns may be sung, and the time concludes with prayers of thanksgiving.

The people and the priest depart with God's blessing

The end of the service is deliberately short but has a powerful meaning. The people are being sent out, dismissed, to go from the service, energized by word and sacrament, to serve God in the world. Here words and action combine. A deacon may speak the words of dismissal, and while many people may actually stop to chat and have some coffee, sharing time together as the community before finally leaving the church, the intention is clear: we are to 'go in peace to love and serve the Lord'.

SHAPE

There are eight Eucharistic Prayers for use with Order One in *Common Worship*. Eucharistic Prayers are rich in language and symbolism, with responsive parts for priest and people. They tell the story of our faith and praise God for his action. They include an *anamnesis* – a memorial of Christ's institution at the Last Supper – so that we 'do this in remembrance of him', and also an *epiclesis* – an invocation upon God the Holy Spirit to continue this work here and now.

Eucharistic Prayer A

This is a putting together and mild revision of the first and second Eucharistic Prayers from the *Alternative Service Book 1980*. Extended Prefaces may be used, replacing all the text between the opening dialogue and the Sanctus (Holy, Holy, Holy). The prayer has its roots in the ancient Western tradition of the early Church.

Eucharistic Prayer B
This prayer is based on the Christian prayer of Hippolytus contained within the Apostolic Tradition, an early liturgical text.

Eucharistic Prayer C
This prayer follows the tradition of the Book of Common Prayer.

Eucharistic Prayer D
This prayer contains many responses and is suitable for services at which children may be present. However, it works well when all ages are able to use it enthusiastically. It is direct and dramatic.

Eucharistic Prayer E
This prayer has a narrative style. There is a very short Preface; the prayer can also be used with extended Prefaces. It is weighted to be petitionary in nature, calling upon God for his help.

Eucharistic Prayer F
This prayer is influenced by the prayer of St Basil, an Eastern Church text dating from the fourth century. In keeping with this tradition, there are no Proper Prefaces but there are congregational acclamations. The prayer is rich and joyful and is good for big occasions.

Eucharistic Prayer G

This different prayer contains the use of paradox, found first in the works of John of the Cross, and also uses feminine imagery, reflecting the gathering in of God's people. There is an opportunity for the insertion of intercession for the Church.

Eucharistic Prayer H

Here the congregation are involved more fully (in terms of spoken responses) than in any other prayer. It is interactive and brief. Again, this prayer is popular when children are present. The prayer ends with the words of the Sanctus, which can be sung as well as said.

In every Eucharist, there is a traditional fourfold shape, mirroring the action of Christ himself at the Last Supper. We *take* the bread and wine, the gifts from among all God has given us and symbols of our offering of ourselves to God. We ask God to *bless* the gifts, using the words Jesus gave us, so that he may be present among us. Just as his body was broken, we *break* the bread to acknowledge our brokenness and dependence on God's forgiveness. And we *share* the bread and wine: Christ's gift of himself to us enables us to share in the life of God, and reminds us that we belong to him and to one another.

SPIRIT

At the Last Supper Jesus gave his disciples signs to remember him by. Following the events of Good Friday and Easter Day, the disciples realized that Jesus had been sharing not just bread and wine but himself, his body and his blood, as a living remembrance of him and his saving work. Every time we celebrate the Eucharist we enter again into the mystery of Christ's sacrifice, as we encounter him in word and sacrament.

The first Christians gathered in one another's homes to celebrate the Eucharist together, often in secret. Christians all over the world still come together to worship in homes, hospitals, churches and cathedrals. In church we gather as individuals, with all our cares and concerns, our joys and sorrows; and in our offering of praise and thanksgiving, Christ makes us one body.

Each time we attend a Eucharist we confess our sins and receive the assurance of God's forgiveness. It is good practice to prepare for this by reflecting beforehand on those ways in which we have failed God or neglected his part in our lives. Then we break open the Scriptures together, and hear anew the story of God's saving acts. We affirm the faith that has been passed on down the centuries, and that we are called to proclaim afresh today. And we bring to God the concerns of the world, the Church, our community, and ourselves – because in the Eucharist we are called to bring all things to God, whose will is to reconcile all things to himself.

At the end of the Eucharist, we are sent out to live as members of the eucharistic community in the world.

Prayer Book for Lay People

The Saviour of the world comes to us in the service no matter how familiar it is, whether or not we feel inspired or holy. As we are fed by him, we are called, once again, to be signs of his love in the world: receiving the body of Christ, we are sent out to *be* the body of Christ.

There is a special day set aside in the Christian year to give thanks for the Eucharist. It is called Corpus Christi, or the Day of Thanksgiving for the Institution of Holy Communion. It falls on the Thursday after Trinity Sunday. Anglicans can use this day to praise God for giving us such a wonderful regular means of grace.

The Eucharist is both a once-and-for-all wonder and a weekly, sometimes even daily, sustenance for the Christian pilgrimage. It may be presented in wholly different ways but the essence is the same: God is with us. The Eucharist is therefore both an earthly gift and a foretaste of heaven. Heaven and earth come close in the celebration of the Eucharist.

THE EUCHARIST

The Gathering

The president may say:

In the name of the Father,
and of the Son,
and of the Holy Spirit.
All   **Amen.**

The Greeting

The Lord be with you
All   **and also with you.**

or

Grace, mercy and peace
from God our Father
and the Lord Jesus Christ
be with you
All   **and also with you.**

From Easter Day to Pentecost this acclamation follows:

Alleluia. Christ is risen.
All   **He is risen indeed. Alleluia.**

Prayer of Preparation

All   **Almighty God,**
to whom all hearts are open,
all desires known,
and from whom no secrets are hidden:
cleanse the thoughts of our hearts
by the inspiration of your Holy Spirit,
that we may perfectly love you,
and worthily magnify your holy name;
through Christ our Lord.
Amen.

Prayers of Penitence

The Commandments, the Beatitudes, the Comfortable Words or
the following Summary of the Law may be used:

Our Lord Jesus Christ said:
The first commandment is this:
'Hear, O Israel, the Lord our God is the only Lord.
You shall love the Lord your God with all your heart,
with all your soul, with all your mind,
and with all your strength.'

The second is this: 'Love your neighbour as yourself.'
There is no other commandment greater than these.
On these two commandments hang all the law and the prophets.

All   **Amen. Lord, have mercy.**

A minister uses a seasonal invitation to confession or these or
other suitable words:

God so loved the world
that he gave his only Son Jesus Christ
to save us from our sins,
to be our advocate in heaven,
and to bring us to eternal life.

Let us confess our sins in penitence and faith,
firmly resolved to keep God's commandments
and to live in love and peace with all.

All   **Almighty God, our heavenly Father,**
we have sinned against you
and against our neighbour
in thought and word and deed,
through negligence, through weakness,
through our own deliberate fault.
We are truly sorry
and repent of all our sins.
For the sake of your Son Jesus Christ,
who died for us,
forgive us all that is past
and grant that we may serve you in newness of life
to the glory of your name.
Amen.

or

All   **Most merciful God,**
Father of our Lord Jesus Christ,
we confess that we have sinned
in thought, word and deed.
We have not loved you with our whole heart.
We have not loved our neighbours as ourselves.
In your mercy
forgive what we have been,

help us to amend what we are,
and direct what we shall be;
that we may do justly,
love mercy,
and walk humbly with you, our God.
Amen.

*Or, with suitable penitential sentences, the Kyrie eleison may
be used:*

Lord, have mercy.
All   **Lord, have mercy.**

Christ, have mercy.
All   **Christ, have mercy.**

Lord, have mercy.
All   **Lord, have mercy.**

*If another confession has already been used, the Kyrie eleison
may be used without interpolation here or after the absolution.*

The president says:

Almighty God,
who forgives all who truly repent,
have mercy upon *you*,
pardon and deliver *you* from all your sins,
confirm and strengthen *you* in all goodness,
and keep *you* in life eternal;
through Jesus Christ our Lord.
All   **Amen.**

Gloria in Excelsis

All   Glory to God in the highest,
and peace to his people on earth.

Lord God, heavenly King,
almighty God and Father,
we worship you, we give you thanks,
we praise you for your glory.

Lord Jesus Christ, only Son of the Father,
Lord God, Lamb of God,
you take away the sin of the world:
have mercy on us;
you are seated at the right hand of the Father:
receive our prayer.

For you alone are the Holy One,
you alone are the Lord,
you alone are the Most High, Jesus Christ,
with the Holy Spirit,
in the glory of God the Father.
Amen.

The Collect

*The president introduces a period of silent prayer with the words
'Let us pray' or a more specific bidding.*

The Collect is said, and all respond:

All   Amen.

The Liturgy of the Word

Readings

Either one or two readings from Scripture precede the Gospel reading.

At the end of each the reader may say:

This is the word of the Lord.

All Thanks be to God.

The psalm or canticle follows the first reading; other hymns and songs may be used between the readings.

Gospel Reading

An acclamation may herald the Gospel reading.

When the Gospel is announced the reader says:

Hear the Gospel of our Lord Jesus Christ according to *N*.

All Glory to you, O Lord.

At the end:

This is the Gospel of the Lord.

All Praise to you, O Christ.

Sermon

The Creed

All   We believe in one God,
the Father, the Almighty,
maker of heaven and earth,
of all that is,
seen and unseen.

We believe in one Lord, Jesus Christ,
the only Son of God,
eternally begotten of the Father,
God from God, Light from Light,
true God from true God,
begotten, not made,
of one Being with the Father;
through him all things were made.
For us and for our salvation he came down from heaven,
was incarnate from the Holy Spirit and the Virgin Mary
and was made man.
For our sake he was crucified under Pontius Pilate;
he suffered death and was buried.
On the third day he rose again
in accordance with the Scriptures;
he ascended into heaven
and is seated at the right hand of the Father.
He will come again in glory to judge the living and the dead,
and his kingdom will have no end.

We believe in the Holy Spirit,
the Lord, the giver of life,
who proceeds from the Father and the Son,
who with the Father and the Son is worshipped and glorified,
who has spoken through the prophets.

We believe in one holy catholic and apostolic Church.
We acknowledge one baptism for the forgiveness of sins.
We look for the resurrection of the dead,
and the life of the world to come.
Amen.

Prayers of Intercession

*The prayers usually include these concerns and may follow this
sequence:*

> *The Church of Christ*
>
> *Creation, human society, the Sovereign and those in authority*
>
> *The local community*
>
> *Those who suffer*
>
> *The communion of saints*

These responses may be used:

Lord, in your mercy
All **hear our prayer.**

or

Lord, hear us.
All **Lord, graciously hear us.**

And at the end:

Merciful Father,
All accept these prayers
for the sake of your Son,
our Saviour Jesus Christ.
Amen.

The Liturgy of the Sacrament

The Peace

The peace of the Lord be always with you
All and also with you.

Let us offer one another a sign of peace.

All may exchange a sign of peace.

Preparation of the Table
Taking of the Bread and Wine

The gifts of the people may be gathered and presented.

The Eucharistic Prayer

Prayer A

The Lord be with you
All **and also with you.**

or

The Lord is here.
All **His Spirit is with us.**

Lift up your hearts.
All **We lift them to the Lord.**

Let us give thanks to the Lord our God.
All **It is right to give thanks and praise.**

It is indeed right,
it is our duty and our joy,
at all times and in all places
to give you thanks and praise,
holy Father, heavenly King,
almighty and eternal God,
through Jesus Christ your Son our Lord.

For he is your living Word;
through him you have created all things from the beginning,
and formed us in your own image.

All **To you be glory and praise for ever.**

Through him you have freed us from the slavery of sin,
giving him to be born of a woman and to die upon the cross;
you raised him from the dead
and exalted him to your right hand on high.

All   **To you be glory and praise for ever.**

Through him you have sent upon us
your holy and life-giving Spirit,
and made us a people for your own possession.

All   **To you be glory and praise for ever.**

Therefore with angels and archangels,
and with all the company of heaven,
we proclaim your great and glorious name,
for ever praising you and *saying*:

All   **Holy, holy, holy Lord,**
God of power and might,
heaven and earth are full of your glory.
Hosanna in the highest.
[Blessed is he who comes in the name of the Lord.
Hosanna in the highest.]

Accept our praises, heavenly Father,
through your Son our Saviour Jesus Christ,
and as we follow his example and obey his command,
grant that by the power of your Holy Spirit
these gifts of bread and wine
may be to us his body and his blood;

who, in the same night that he was betrayed,
took bread and gave you thanks;
he broke it and gave it to his disciples, saying:

Take, eat; this is my body which is given for you;
do this in remembrance of me.

All **To you be glory and praise for ever.**

In the same way, after supper
he took the cup and gave you thanks;
he gave it to them, saying:
Drink this, all of you;
this is my blood of the new covenant,
which is shed for you and for many for the forgiveness of sins.
Do this, as often as you drink it,
in remembrance of me.

All **To you be glory and praise for ever.**

Therefore, heavenly Father,
we remember his offering of himself
made once for all upon the cross;
we proclaim his mighty resurrection and glorious ascension;
we look for the coming of your kingdom,
and with this bread and this cup
we make the memorial of Christ your Son our Lord.

One of these four acclamations is used:

[Great is the mystery of faith:]
All **Christ has died:**
Christ is risen:
Christ will come again.

[Praise to you, Lord Jesus:]
All **Dying you destroyed our death,**
rising you restored our life:
Lord Jesus, come in glory.

[Christ is the bread of life:]
All **When we eat this bread and drink this cup,
we proclaim your death, Lord Jesus,
until you come in glory.**

[Jesus Christ is Lord:]
All **Lord, by your cross and resurrection
you have set us free.
You are the Saviour of the world.**

Accept through him, our great high priest,
this our sacrifice of thanks and praise,
and as we eat and drink these holy gifts
in the presence of your divine majesty,
renew us by your Spirit,
inspire us with your love
and unite us in the body of your Son,
Jesus Christ our Lord.

All **To you be glory and praise for ever.**

Through him, and with him, and in him,
in the unity of the Holy Spirit,
with all who stand before you in earth and heaven,
we worship you, Father almighty,
in songs of everlasting praise:

All **Blessing and honour and glory and power
be yours for ever and ever. Amen.**

The service continues with the Lord's Prayer on page 55.

Prayer B

The Lord be with you
All **and also with you.**

or

The Lord is here.
All **His Spirit is with us.**

Lift up your hearts.
All **We lift them to the Lord.**

Let us give thanks to the Lord our God.
All **It is right to give thanks and praise.**

Father, we give you thanks and praise
through your beloved Son Jesus Christ, your living Word,
through whom you have created all things;
who was sent by you in your great goodness to be our Saviour.

By the power of the Holy Spirit he took flesh;
as your Son, born of the blessed Virgin,
he lived on earth and went about among us;
he opened wide his arms for us on the cross;
he put an end to death by dying for us;
and revealed the resurrection by rising to new life;
so he fulfilled your will and won for you a holy people.

Therefore with angels and archangels,
and with all the company of heaven,
we proclaim your great and glorious name,
for ever praising you and *saying*:

All Holy, holy, holy Lord,
   God of power and might,
   heaven and earth are full of your glory.
   Hosanna in the highest.
   [Blessed is he who comes in the name of the Lord.
   Hosanna in the highest.]

   Lord, you are holy indeed, the source of all holiness;
   grant that by the power of your Holy Spirit,
   and according to your holy will,
   these gifts of bread and wine
   may be to us the body and blood of our Lord Jesus Christ;

   who, in the same night that he was betrayed,
   took bread and gave you thanks;
   he broke it and gave it to his disciples, saying:
   Take, eat; this is my body which is given for you;
   do this in remembrance of me.

   In the same way, after supper
   he took the cup and gave you thanks;
   he gave it to them, saying:
   Drink this, all of you;
   this is my blood of the new covenant,
   which is shed for you and for many for the forgiveness of sins.
   Do this, as often as you drink it,
   in remembrance of me.

   One of these four acclamations is used:

   [Great is the mystery of faith:]
All **Christ has died:**
   Christ is risen:
   Christ will come again.

[Praise to you, Lord Jesus:]
All **Dying you destroyed our death,**
rising you restored our life:
Lord Jesus, come in glory.

[Christ is the bread of life:]
All **When we eat this bread and drink this cup,**
we proclaim your death,
Lord Jesus, until you come in glory.

[Jesus Christ is Lord:]
All **Lord, by your cross and resurrection**
you have set us free.
You are the Saviour of the world.

And so, Father, calling to mind his death on the cross,
his perfect sacrifice made once for the sins of the whole world;
rejoicing in his mighty resurrection and glorious ascension,
and looking for his coming in glory,
we celebrate this memorial of our redemption.
As we offer you this our sacrifice of praise and thanksgiving,
we bring before you this bread and this cup
and we thank you for counting us worthy
to stand in your presence and serve you.

Send the Holy Spirit on your people
and gather into one in your kingdom
all who share this one bread and one cup,
so that we, in the company of [*N and*] all the saints,
may praise and glorify you for ever,
through Jesus Christ our Lord;

by whom, and with whom, and in whom,
in the unity of the Holy Spirit,
all honour and glory be yours, almighty Father,
for ever and ever.

All   **Amen.**

The service continues with the Lord's Prayer on page 55.

Prayer C

The Lord be with you
All   **and also with you.**

or

The Lord is here.
All   **His Spirit is with us.**

Lift up your hearts.
All   **We lift them to the Lord.**

Let us give thanks to the Lord our God.
All   **It is right to give thanks and praise.**

It is indeed right,
it is our duty and our joy,
at all times and in all places
to give you thanks and praise,
holy Father, heavenly King,
almighty and eternal God,
through Jesus Christ our Lord.

Short Proper Preface, or

For he is our great high priest,
who has loosed us from our sins
and has made us to be a royal priesthood to you,
our God and Father.

Therefore with angels and archangels,
and with all the company of heaven,
we proclaim your great and glorious name,
for ever praising you and *saying*:

All   **Holy, holy, holy Lord,
God of power and might,
heaven and earth are full of your glory.
Hosanna in the highest.
[Blessed is he who comes in the name of the Lord.
Hosanna in the highest.]**

All glory be to you, our heavenly Father,
who, in your tender mercy,
gave your only Son our Saviour Jesus Christ
to suffer death upon the cross for our redemption;
who made there by his one oblation of himself once offered
a full, perfect and sufficient sacrifice, oblation and satisfaction
   for the sins of the whole world;
he instituted, and in his holy gospel commanded us to continue,
a perpetual memory of his precious death until he comes again.

Hear us, merciful Father, we humbly pray,
and grant that, by the power of your Holy Spirit,
we receiving these gifts of your creation, this bread and this wine,
according to your Son our Saviour Jesus Christ's holy institution,
in remembrance of his death and passion,
may be partakers of his most blessed body and blood;

who, in the same night that he was betrayed,
took bread and gave you thanks;
he broke it and gave it to his disciples, saying:
Take, eat; this is my body which is given for you;
do this in remembrance of me.

In the same way, after supper
he took the cup and gave you thanks;
he gave it to them, saying:
Drink this, all of you;
this is my blood of the new covenant,
which is shed for you and for many for the forgiveness of sins.
Do this, as often as you drink it,
in remembrance of me.

One of these four acclamations is used:

[Great is the mystery of faith:]
All   **Christ has died:**
Christ is risen:
Christ will come again.

[Praise to you, Lord Jesus:]
All   **Dying you destroyed our death,**
rising you restored our life:
Lord Jesus, come in glory.

[Christ is the bread of life:]
All   **When we eat this bread and drink this cup,**
we proclaim your death,
Lord Jesus, until you come in glory.

[Jesus Christ is Lord:]

All **Lord, by your cross and resurrection
you have set us free.
You are the Saviour of the world.**

Therefore, Lord and heavenly Father,
in remembrance of the precious death and passion,
the mighty resurrection and glorious ascension
of your dear Son Jesus Christ,
we offer you through him this our sacrifice of praise
    and thanksgiving.

Grant that by his merits and death,
and through faith in his blood,
we and all your Church may receive forgiveness of our sins
and all other benefits of his passion.
Although we are unworthy, through our manifold sins,
to offer you any sacrifice,
yet we pray that you will accept this
the duty and service that we owe.
Do not weigh our merits, but pardon our offences,
and fill us all who share in this holy communion
with your grace and heavenly blessing;

through Jesus Christ our Lord,
by whom, and with whom, and in whom,
in the unity of the Holy Spirit,
all honour and glory be yours, almighty Father,
for ever and ever.

All **Amen.**

The service continues with the Lord's Prayer on page 55.

Prayer D

The Lord be with you
All   **and also with you.**

or

The Lord is here.
All   **His Spirit is with us.**

Lift up your hearts.
All   **We lift them to the Lord.**

Let us give thanks to the Lord our God.
All   **It is right to give thanks and praise.**

Almighty God, good Father to us all,
your face is turned towards your world.
In love you gave us Jesus your Son
to rescue us from sin and death.
Your Word goes out to call us home
    to the city where angels sing your praise.
We join with them in heaven's song:

All   **Holy, holy, holy Lord,**
God of power and might,
heaven and earth are full of your glory.
Hosanna in the highest.
[Blessed is he who comes in the name of the Lord.
Hosanna in the highest.]

Father of all, we give you thanks
    for every gift that comes from heaven.

To the darkness Jesus came as your light.
With signs of faith and words of hope
he touched untouchables with love and washed the guilty clean.

This is his story.

All **This is our song:**
Hosanna in the highest.

The crowds came out to see your Son,
   yet at the end they turned on him.
On the night he was betrayed
he came to table with his friends
   to celebrate the freedom of your people.

This is his story.

All **This is our song:**
Hosanna in the highest.

Jesus blessed you, Father, for the food;
he took bread, gave thanks, broke it and said:
This is my body, given for you all.
Jesus then gave thanks for the wine;
he took the cup, gave it and said:
This is my blood, shed for you all
   for the forgiveness of sins.
Do this in remembrance of me.

This is our story.

All **This is our song:**
Hosanna in the highest.

Therefore, Father, with this bread and this cup
we celebrate the cross
on which he died to set us free.
Defying death he rose again
and is alive with you to plead for us and all the world.

This is our story.

All **This is our song:**
Hosanna in the highest.

Send your Spirit on us now
that by these gifts we may feed on Christ
    with opened eyes and hearts on fire.

May we and all who share this food
offer ourselves to live for you
and be welcomed at your feast in heaven
    where all creation worships you,
Father, Son and Holy Spirit:

All **Blessing and honour and glory and power**
be yours for ever and ever.
Amen.

The service continues with the Lord's Prayer on page 55.

Prayer E

The Lord be with you
All **and also with you.**

or

The Lord is here.
All **His Spirit is with us.**

Lift up your hearts.
All **We lift them to the Lord.**

Let us give thanks to the Lord our God.
All **It is right to give thanks and praise.**

Father, you made the world and love your creation.
You gave your Son Jesus Christ to be our Saviour.
His dying and rising have set us free from sin and death.
And so we gladly thank you,
with saints and angels praising you, and *saying*:

All **Holy, holy, holy Lord,**
God of power and might,
heaven and earth are full of your glory.
Hosanna in the highest.
[Blessed is he who comes in the name of the Lord.
Hosanna in the highest.]

We praise and bless you, loving Father,
through Jesus Christ, our Lord;
and as we obey his command,
send your Holy Spirit,
that broken bread and wine outpoured
may be for us the body and blood of your dear Son.

On the night before he died he had supper with his friends
and, taking bread, he praised you.
He broke the bread, gave it to them and said:
Take, eat; this is my body which is given for you;
do this in remembrance of me.

When supper was ended he took the cup of wine.
Again he praised you, gave it to them and said:
Drink this, all of you;
this is my blood of the new covenant,
which is shed for you and for many for the forgiveness of sins.
Do this, as often as you drink it, in remembrance of me.

So, Father, we remember all that Jesus did,
in him we plead with confidence his sacrifice
made once for all upon the cross.

Bringing before you the bread of life and cup of salvation,
we proclaim his death and resurrection
until he comes in glory.

One of these four acclamations is used:

[Great is the mystery of faith:]

All **Christ has died:**
Christ is risen:
Christ will come again.

[Praise to you, Lord Jesus:]

All **Dying you destroyed our death,**
rising you restored our life:
Lord Jesus, come in glory.

[Christ is the bread of life:]

All **When we eat this bread and drink this cup,**
we proclaim your death,
Lord Jesus, until you come in glory.

[Jesus Christ is Lord:]

All **Lord, by your cross and resurrection**
you have set us free.
You are the Saviour of the world.

Lord of all life,
help us to work together for that day
when your kingdom comes
and justice and mercy will be seen in all the earth.

Look with favour on your people,
gather us in your loving arms
and bring us with [*N and*] all the saints
to feast at your table in heaven.

Through Christ, and with Christ, and in Christ,
in the unity of the Holy Spirit,
all honour and glory are yours, O loving Father,
for ever and ever.
Amen.

The service continues with the Lord's Prayer on page 55.

Prayer F

The Lord be with you
All **and also with you.**

or

The Lord is here.
All **His Spirit is with us.**

Lift up your hearts.
All **We lift them to the Lord.**

Let us give thanks to the Lord our God.
All **It is right to give thanks and praise.**

You are worthy of our thanks and praise,
Lord God of truth,
for by the breath of your mouth
you have spoken your word,
and all things have come into being.

You fashioned us in your image
and placed us in the garden of your delight.
Though we chose the path of rebellion
you would not abandon your own.

Again and again you drew us into your covenant of grace.
You gave your people the law and taught us by your prophets
to look for your reign of justice, mercy and peace.

As we watch for the signs of your kingdom on earth,
we echo the song of the angels in heaven,
evermore praising you and *saying*:

All   **Holy, holy, holy Lord,
God of power and might,
heaven and earth are full of your glory.
Hosanna in the highest.
[Blessed is he who comes in the name of the Lord.
Hosanna in the highest.]**

Lord God, you are the most holy one,
enthroned in splendour and light,
yet in the coming of your Son Jesus Christ
you reveal the power of your love
made perfect in our human weakness.

[*All*   **Amen. Lord, we believe.**]

Embracing our humanity,
Jesus showed us the way of salvation;
loving us to the end,
he gave himself to death for us;
dying for his own,
he set us free from the bonds of sin,
that we might rise and reign with him in glory.

[*All*   **Amen. Lord, we believe.**]

On the night he gave up himself for us all
he took bread and gave you thanks;
he broke it and gave it to his disciples, saying:
Take, eat; this is my body which is given for you;
do this in remembrance of me.

[*All*   **Amen. Lord, we believe.**]

In the same way, after supper
he took the cup and gave you thanks;
he gave it to them, saying:
Drink this, all of you; this is my blood of the new covenant
which is shed for you and for many for the forgiveness of sins.
Do this, as often as you drink it, in remembrance of me.

[*All*   **Amen. Lord, we believe.**]

Therefore we proclaim the death that he suffered on the cross,
we celebrate his resurrection, his bursting from the tomb,
we rejoice that he reigns at your right hand on high
and we long for his coming in glory.

[*All*   **Amen. Come, Lord Jesus.**]

As we recall the one, perfect sacrifice of our redemption,
Father, by your Holy Spirit let these gifts of your creation
be to us the body and blood of our Lord Jesus Christ;
form us into the likeness of Christ
and make us a perfect offering in your sight.

[*All*   Amen. Come, Holy Spirit.]

Look with favour on your people
and in your mercy hear the cry of our hearts.
Bless the earth,
heal the sick,
let the oppressed go free
and fill your Church with power from on high.

[*All*   Amen. Come, Holy Spirit.]

Gather your people from the ends of the earth
to feast with [*N and*] all your saints
at the table in your kingdom,
where the new creation is brought to perfection
in Jesus Christ our Lord;

by whom, and with whom, and in whom,
in the unity of the Holy Spirit,
all honour and glory be yours, almighty Father,
for ever and ever.

All   Amen.

The service continues with the Lord's Prayer on page 55.

Prayer G

The Lord be with you
All **and also with you.**

or

The Lord is here.
All **His Spirit is with us.**

Lift up your hearts.
All **We lift them to the Lord.**

Let us give thanks to the Lord our God.
All **It is right to give thanks and praise.**

Blessed are you, Lord God,
our light and our salvation;
to you be glory and praise for ever.

From the beginning you have created all things
and all your works echo the silent music of your praise.
In the fullness of time you made us in your image,
the crown of all creation.

You give us breath and speech, that with angels and archangels
and all the powers of heaven
we may find a voice to sing your praise:

All **Holy, holy, holy Lord,**
God of power and might,
heaven and earth are full of your glory.
Hosanna in the highest.
[Blessed is he who comes in the name of the Lord.
Hosanna in the highest.]

How wonderful the work of your hands, O Lord.
As a mother tenderly gathers her children,
you embraced a people as your own.
When they turned away and rebelled
your love remained steadfast.

From them you raised up Jesus our Saviour, born of Mary,
to be the living bread,
in whom all our hungers are satisfied.

He offered his life for sinners,
and with a love stronger than death
he opened wide his arms on the cross.

On the night before he died,
he came to supper with his friends
and, taking bread, he gave you thanks.
He broke it and gave it to them, saying:
Take, eat; this is my body which is given for you;
do this in remembrance of me.

At the end of supper, taking the cup of wine,
he gave you thanks, and said:
Drink this, all of you; this is my blood of the new covenant,
which is shed for you and for many for the forgiveness of sins.
Do this, as often as you drink it, in remembrance of me.

One of these four acclamations is used:

[Great is the mystery of faith:]
All　**Christ has died:**
Christ is risen:
Christ will come again.

[Praise to you, Lord Jesus:]
All   **Dying you destroyed our death,**
rising you restored our life:
Lord Jesus, come in glory.

[Christ is the bread of life:]
All   **When we eat this bread and drink this cup,**
we proclaim your death,
Lord Jesus, until you come in glory.

[Jesus Christ is Lord:]
All   **Lord, by your cross and resurrection**
you have set us free.
You are the Saviour of the world.

Father, we plead with confidence
his sacrifice made once for all upon the cross;
we remember his dying and rising in glory,
and we rejoice that he intercedes for us at your right hand.

Pour out your Holy Spirit as we bring before you
these gifts of your creation;
may they be for us the body and blood of your dear Son.

As we eat and drink these holy things in your presence,
form us in the likeness of Christ,
and build us into a living temple to your glory.

[Remember, Lord, your Church in every land.
Reveal her unity, guard her faith,
and preserve her in peace . . .]

Bring us at the last with [*N and*] all the saints
to the vision of that eternal splendour
for which you have created us;
through Jesus Christ, our Lord,
by whom, with whom, and in whom,
with all who stand before you in earth and heaven,
we worship you, Father almighty, in songs of everlasting praise:

All **Blessing and honour and glory and power
be yours for ever and ever.
Amen.**

The service continues with the Lord's Prayer on page 55.
.

Prayer H

The Lord be with you
All **and also with you.**

or

The Lord is here.
All **His Spirit is with us.**

Lift up your hearts.
All **We lift them to the Lord.**

Let us give thanks to the Lord our God.
All **It is right to give thanks and praise.**

It is right to praise you, Father, Lord of all creation;
in your love you made us for yourself.

When we turned away
you did not reject us,
but came to meet us in your Son.

All **You embraced us as your children
and welcomed us to sit and eat with you.**

In Christ you shared our life
that we might live in him and he in us.

All **He opened his arms of love upon the cross
and made for all the perfect sacrifice for sin.**

On the night he was betrayed,
at supper with his friends
he took bread, and gave you thanks;
he broke it and gave it to them, saying:
Take, eat; this is my body which is given for you;
do this in remembrance of me.

All **Father, we do this in remembrance of him:
his body is the bread of life.**

At the end of supper, taking the cup of wine,
he gave you thanks, and said:
Drink this, all of you; this is my blood of the new covenant,
which is shed for you for the forgiveness of sins;
do this in remembrance of me.

All **Father, we do this in remembrance of him:
his blood is shed for all.**

As we proclaim his death and celebrate his rising in glory,
send your Holy Spirit that this bread and this wine
may be to us the body and blood of your dear Son.

All **As we eat and drink these holy gifts
make us one in Christ, our risen Lord.**

With your whole Church throughout the world
we offer you this sacrifice of praise
and lift our voice to join the eternal song of heaven:

All   Holy, holy, holy Lord,
God of power and might,
Heaven and earth are full of your glory.
Hosanna in the highest.

The service continues with the Lord's Prayer.

The Lord's Prayer

As our Saviour taught us, so we pray

All   Our Father in heaven,
hallowed be your name,
your kingdom come,
your will be done,
on earth as in heaven.
Give us today our daily bread.
Forgive us our sins
as we forgive those who sin against us.
Lead us not into temptation
but deliver us from evil.
For the kingdom, the power,
and the glory are yours
now and for ever.
Amen.

or

Let us pray with confidence as our Saviour has taught us

All   Our Father, who art in heaven,
hallowed be thy name;
thy kingdom come;
thy will be done;
on earth as it is in heaven.
Give us this day our daily bread.
And forgive us our trespasses,
as we forgive those who trespass against us.
And lead us not into temptation;
but deliver us from evil.
For thine is the kingdom,
the power and the glory,
for ever and ever.
Amen.

Breaking of the Bread

The president breaks the consecrated bread.

We break this bread
to share in the body of Christ.
All   Though we are many, we are one body,
because we all share in one bread.

or

Every time we eat this bread
and drink this cup,
All   we proclaim the Lord's death
until he comes.

The Agnus Dei may be used as the bread is broken.

All   Lamb of God,
you take away the sin of the world,
have mercy on us.

Lamb of God,
you take away the sin of the world,
have mercy on us.

Lamb of God,
you take away the sin of the world,
grant us peace.

or

All   Jesus, Lamb of God,
have mercy on us.

Jesus, bearer of our sins,
have mercy on us.

Jesus, redeemer of the world,
grant us peace.

Giving of Communion

The president says one of these invitations to communion:

Draw near with faith.
Receive the body of our Lord Jesus Christ
which he gave for you,
and his blood which he shed for you.
Eat and drink
in remembrance that he died for you,
and feed on him in your hearts
by faith with thanksgiving.

or

Jesus is the Lamb of God
who takes away the sin of the world.
Blessed are those who are called to his supper.

All   Lord, I am not worthy to receive you,
but only say the word, and I shall be healed.

or

God's holy gifts
for God's holy people.

All   Jesus Christ is holy,
Jesus Christ is Lord,
to the glory of God the Father.

One of these prayers may be said before the distribution:

All   We do not presume
to come to this your table, merciful Lord,
trusting in our own righteousness,
but in your manifold and great mercies.
We are not worthy
so much as to gather up the crumbs under your table.
But you are the same Lord
whose nature is always to have mercy.
Grant us therefore, gracious Lord,
so to eat the flesh of your dear Son Jesus Christ
and to drink his blood,
that our sinful bodies may be made clean by his body
and our souls washed through his most precious blood,
and that we may evermore dwell in him, and he in us.
Amen.

All Most merciful Lord,
your love compels us to come in.
Our hands were unclean,
our hearts were unprepared;
we were not fit
even to eat the crumbs from under your table.
But you, Lord, are the God of our salvation,
and share your bread with sinners.
So cleanse and feed us
with the precious body and blood of your Son,
that he may live in us and we in him;
and that we, with the whole company of Christ,
may sit and eat in your kingdom.
Amen.

The president and people receive communion. Each person,
on receiving the elements, says
Amen.

Prayer after Communion

Silence is kept.

The Post Communion or another suitable prayer is said.

All may say one of these prayers:

All Almighty God,
we thank you for feeding us
with the body and blood of your Son Jesus Christ.
Through him we offer you our souls and bodies
to be a living sacrifice.
Send us out
in the power of your Spirit

to live and work
to your praise and glory.
Amen.

or

All   Father of all,
we give you thanks and praise,
that when we were still far off
you met us in your Son and brought us home.
Dying and living, he declared your love,
gave us grace, and opened the gate of glory.
May we who share Christ's body live his risen life;
we who drink his cup bring life to others;
we whom the Spirit lights give light to the world.
Keep us firm in the hope you have set before us,
so we and all your children shall be free,
and the whole earth live to praise your name;
through Christ our Lord.
Amen.

The Dismissal

The president may use a seasonal blessing, or another suitable blessing.

or

The peace of God,
which passes all understanding,
keep your hearts and minds
in the knowledge and love of God,
and of his Son Jesus Christ our Lord;

and the blessing of God almighty,
the Father, the Son, and the Holy Spirit,
be among you and remain with you always.

All **Amen.**

A minister says:

Go in peace to love and serve the Lord.

All **In the name of Christ. Amen.**

or

Go in the peace of Christ.

All **Thanks be to God.**

or, from Easter Day to Pentecost:

Go in the peace of Christ. Alleluia, alleluia.

All **Thanks be to God. Alleluia, alleluia.**

HOLY COMMUNION
AT HOME OR IN HOSPITAL

Whether at home, in hospital, whether because of illness or infirmity, or because of joy or celebration, receiving communion personally or in a small group is a uniquely special and humbling moment.

What should someone expect when they are to receive communion at home or in hospital?

STRUCTURE

Common Worship provides services for the Celebration of Holy Communion at Home or in a Hospital and for the Distribution of Holy Communion at Home or in Hospital. The former is for when the Communion service can be celebrated there and then, perhaps for a small group in a residential home or simply for one individual in particular need, and the latter is for when the visit demands that the previously consecrated bread and wine are taken to the person. Each and every situation will have its own pastoral circumstances that will dictate the content, formality/informality and the duration of the time of worship. *Common Worship* provides modern-language and traditional-language versions of each service.

Usually, only one Scripture reading is used, and that should always be a Gospel reading, properly the reading for the previous Sunday. The length of the service can be varied by the minister according to the pastoral circumstances and degree of participation, especially if the people's spoken parts are a challenge for the participant. Joining in is welcomed at whatever level is manageable. The ministry of the laying on of hands with prayer and anointing should only be used if required, and always with prior agreement. It should be remembered that such a celebration is not less valid, or of less spiritual value, just because it takes place in a home or in hospital and not in a church.

SHAPE

The priest will usually want to make an appointment for such a visit. Some people, especially at home, like to make preparations for the visit by spending some time beforehand in quiet prayer or reading the other Bible passages for the day or for the week. This ministry has to be entirely flexible. You may like to prepare a space on a table, perhaps with a suitable white cloth and candle or cross nearby. Any visitors may join in if they so wish. Light conversation often helps to put everyone at ease. A card with the words of the liturgy will be provided by the minister.

In hospital, things can be somewhat more difficult to prepare, but it is important to remember that hospital staff and clergy are used to this happening and will not feel as self-conscious as the patient. It is often good to pull bedside curtains around a bed to avoid offence to others, but this should always be checked first with staff. The patient must not feel it necessary to change position or 'try harder' just because of this visit. In all situations, God can cope with the pastoral necessities, and all that matters is that the service is taking place.

When a person at home or a patient in hospital cannot receive communion in both kinds, that is, both the consecrated bread and the wine, then receiving in one kind is still receiving communion in all its fullness. Jesus does not share half of himself. Similarly, those who are not well enough to receive the sacrament can be reassured that they are receiving, by faith, the body and the blood of Christ and, by them, the benefits that he gives to us.

SPIRIT

'I was sick and you took care of me, I was in prison and you visited me' (Matthew 25.36). Jesus taught us the importance of visiting. In this service, Jesus himself visits us in the form of Scripture, bread and wine. Often there is an element of dehumanization about being ill or housebound. So there is also a social element to such visiting. Meeting with someone is personal, touching and holy. It is important, each month, to share time, to share news, to share prayer, to share Scripture, to share bread and wine, to share Jesus.

The service given in this book is for the distribution (giving) of Holy Communion at home when the bread and wine have already been consecrated.

HOLY COMMUNION
AT HOME OR IN HOSPITAL

The Greeting

Peace be to this house and to all who live in it.

Words of Introduction

If the bread and wine have been consecrated earlier, the minister says:

The Church of God, of which we are members, has taken bread and wine and given thanks over them according to our Lord's command. These holy gifts are now offered to us that, with faith and thanksgiving, we may share in the communion of the body and blood of Christ.

**Almighty God,
to whom all hearts are open,
all desires known,
and from whom no secrets are hidden:
cleanse the thoughts of our hearts
by the inspiration of your Holy Spirit,
that we may perfectly love you,
and worthily magnify your holy name;
through Christ our Lord.
Amen.**

Come to me all who labour and are heavy laden,
and I will give you rest.

God shows his love for us
in that when we were still sinners, Christ died for us.
let us then show our love for him
by confessing our sins in penitence and faith.

**Almighty God, our heavenly Father,
we have sinned against you
and against our neighbour
in thought and word and deed,
through negligence, through weakness,
through our own deliberate fault.
We are truly sorry
and repent of all our sins.
For the sake of your Son Jesus Christ,
who died for us, forgive us all that is past,
and grant that we may serve you in newness of life
to the glory of your name.
Amen.**

The president says the Absolution.

The Collect

Reading(s) and Prayers

Laying on of Hands and Anointing

The Peace

The president may say

The peace of the Lord be always with you
and also with you.

The Lord's Prayer

Invitation to Communion

Prayer of Humble Access

We do not presume
to come to this your table, merciful Lord,
trusting in our own righteousness,
but in your manifold and great mercies.
We are not worthy
so much as to gather up the crumbs under your table.
But you are the same Lord
whose nature is always to have mercy.
Grant us, therefore, gracious Lord,
so to eat the flesh of your dear Son Jesus Christ
and to drink his blood,
that our sinful bodies may be made clean by his body
and our souls washed through his most precious blood,
and that we may evermore dwell in him, and he in us.
Amen.

Giving of Communion

When the elements are given, the communicant says

Amen.

Prayer after Communion

All   Almighty God,
we thank you for feeding us
with the body and blood of your Son Jesus Christ.
Through him we offer you our souls and bodies
to be a living sacrifice.
Strengthen us
in the power of your Spirit
to live and work
to your praise and glory.
Amen.

The Grace or a Blessing

THE CHURCH'S YEAR

The Church's Year, also called the Church's Calendar, is the route map for the Christian journey. If we understand the truth of Christ to be the same yesterday, today and for ever, then the telling and retelling of the good news celebrate his continuing presence and activity in the world. Following the Church's Year not only articulates the Christian story and encourages observance, but also promotes an ever-deepening awareness of how God is involved in our daily lives. *Common Worship* provides a calendar that is faithful to the wider Christian tradition and emphasizes the Church of England's particular heritage.

The celebration of the Church's Year helps teach the faith. Throughout the year, the ebb and flow of life finds anchor points through the rehearsal of our salvation history. We are able to interpret the ups and downs of life through our understanding of the story. This is reflected too in the natural passage of the seasons and the human experience of living in a real world.

STRUCTURE

If many of the *Common Worship* services provide a clear structure, then the Church's Year is the structure *par excellence*. For the dedicated Christian, the structure of life is shaped by the Church's Year. Meaning and content become more important than simply the passage of time.

The Church's Year begins on Advent Sunday. Throughout the year, each Sunday celebrates the paschal mystery of the death and resurrection of the Lord, with the theme of the season. There are two cycles within the year: the Incarnation cycle and the Eastertide cycle. The Incarnation cycle runs from Advent Sunday to the Feast of the Presentation of Christ in the Temple (Candlemas 2 February). The Easter cycle begins on Ash Wednesday and concludes on the Feast of Pentecost. The rest of the year is mostly designated as Ordinary Time, Sundays without specific seasonal emphases. After Pentecost these are called Sundays after Trinity.

There are Principal Feasts within this framework that are staging posts for the Christian journey. The Principal Feasts in *Common Worship* are:

- Christmas Day
- The Epiphany
- The Presentation of Christ in the Temple
- The Annunciation of Our Lord to the Blessed Virgin Mary
- Easter Day

- Ascension Day
- Pentecost (Whit Sunday)
- Trinity Sunday
- All Saints' Day

On these days Holy Communion should be celebrated in every cathedral and parish church.

The other Principal Holy Days are Ash Wednesday, Maundy Thursday and Good Friday. The Christian Year ends with the Sunday next before Advent, the Feast of Christ the King.

SHAPE

The Church's Year is given shape by the way in which we celebrate these special days and seasons. Through colour, decoration, music, words and symbol we give depth and perspective to our worship. Indeed, the *Common Worship* book that describes the Church's Year in greatest detail is appropriately entitled *Times and Seasons*. Churches use these seasonal and special day provisions in different ways. One of the joys of the Church of England is the broad range of ways in which worship is represented. However, there are familiar ways of marking these seasons and days. Music and hymn singing is probably the most obvious way in which to set a tone for an act of worship. At Christmas we sing carols, at Easter we sing Alleluias. Whether led by organ and robed choir or worship band and amplifier, it is possible and desirable that what we sing expresses the Church's Year just as much as what we say in a service. Indeed, it is music and singing that speak to the heart perhaps more than any spoken word.

Common Worship provides rich resources that bring together the themes and essential theological descriptions for days and seasons. These are placed within the structure of a service and may appropriately include words of introduction to prayers of penitence or before the exchange of the Peace. Such texts are often called 'Propers'. Seasonal Prefaces to certain Eucharistic Prayers may not be printed in every order of service but they are often spoken by the president, and these give wonderful accounts of God acting in our world. Special words of blessing and other texts give *texture* to the *Common Worship* services.

Our churches in England are often beautiful places in themselves, but on special days, such as Easter and for the following season, flowers and other decorations, such as banners or tapestries, can give artistic expression to our offering of worship. Similarly, the absence of colour and light or the simple exercise of restraint can help us comprehend the mood of the day or season, for example, during Lent.

The most visible way in which expression is given to our worship is through liturgical colours. Appropriate liturgical colours for hangings and vestments are suggested in *Common Worship*. They are not mandatory and may reflect local use, but most churches find it helpful to make the use of liturgical colours an aspect of their worship. After all, we do that ourselves in the way in which we dress for sombre or happy occasions. Here is a brief summary of the colours used for liturgical purposes.

- *White* is the colour for days and seasons of great celebration, such as All Saints' Day or Eastertide. Gold can replace white for unique days, such as Christmas and Easter. White is the colour of purity and new beginnings. White vestments are also worn for saints not venerated as martyrs, and in Holy Baptism. White is used for marriages and other pastoral situations as the moment suggests. White (or gold) is seen as the 'best' colour.
- *Red* is used during Holy Week (although white is used on Maundy Thursday). Red is the colour of blood and fire and so is used on the Feast of Pentecost and for those saints who were killed for their faith, the martyrs. Red is the most appropriate colour when the focus is on the gift of the Holy Spirit and so is often used in Confirmation and Ordination.
- *Purple* is the colour for Advent and Lent (although some places may have the tradition of unbleached linen for the 40 days of Lent). Purple is recommended for most funerals. It is a colour of dignity, respect and penitence.
- *Green* is used for Ordinary Time. The colour of much of life, it expresses that God in the everyday is anything but ordinary, and is wonderful in his creation.

Symbols – such as the Advent Wreath and the Paschal Candle – are often used to give further expression to the Christian Year. Unimportant in themselves, they give our worship a focus as one day succeeds another. A brief overview of the Christian Year will help us to see how this narrative comes to life.

Advent begins the year with four Sundays of preparation for the coming of Christ at Christmas. The word 'advent' means 'coming'. While the rest of society is deeply immersed in its consumerist extravaganza, the Church seeks to prepare itself properly for the incarnation. The Advent Wreath may be used to 'count down' the four Sundays, and seasonal prayers and Propers help us to understand the importance of God acting through human history until the dramatic 'advent' of our Lord. The Gloria is not sung during Advent.

Christmas is characterized by a powerful shift in mood with the joyful singing of carols, the building of the crib scene and proclamations that the Word has been made flesh.

Epiphany is part of the Incarnation cycle and tells of how we come to recognize Jesus for who he really is. The Magi join the crib scene (as the shepherds go back to their work) and we reflect on the baptism of Jesus and the wedding at Cana in Galilee. The word 'epiphany' means 'manifestation': it signifies our gradual realization that God's Son is manifest in the world. Epiphany is a good example of a particular day that is part of a season that is itself part of a greater cycle within the Church's Year.

Candlemas is a day that marks the end of the Incarnation cycle. It is recognized by the carrying of candles in procession as the Christ child was carried into the Temple and recognized as the Light of the World.

Ash Wednesday is the start of the Lent season, during which we remember Jesus being tempted in the wilderness, and which ends with our commemoration of his Passion and death. The name Ash Wednesday comes from the ancient penitential practice known as the Imposition of Ashes, when the sign of the cross in ash (from burnt palm crosses) is made on the forehead of each person. This is a powerful reminder of our mortality, the ash symbolizing the dust from which we come and to which we shall return, and reminding us that through this time in the 'wilderness' we look towards the cross. The Gloria is not sung during Lent.

Holy Week is the most dramatic of times for Christians as we walk the way of the cross with Christ. On Palm Sunday Holy Communion has two distinct themes: there is the triumphant entry into Jerusalem, often accompanied by a procession with branches to the church; then the painful moment as the Passion Gospel is read (often dramatically with different voice parts) when the crowd turn on Jesus and he is condemned.

Maundy Thursday marks the Last Supper, the Passover meal at which Jesus instituted the Eucharist. As a sign of his love for them and his calling for them to serve, he washed the disciples' feet, and during the service the president may re-enact this moving Gospel account. After the meal Jesus goes into the night to the Garden of Gethsemane where his agony over what is to come is exacerbated by the weakness of his disciples. Often a watch is kept until midnight and the church is stripped of all decoration. On Good Friday the focus is placed upon the cross, sometimes in a three-hour service, marking the time Jesus hung upon the cross. Different churches have different customs about receiving communion on this day.

Easter begins with either a vigil service or a dawn service as we celebrate the resurrection from death of the Saviour of the world. Like the birth, the resurrection took place at night as light broke into darkness. When the disciples came to the tomb at dawn, they found the stone already rolled away. The Easter ceremonies include a vigil of readings telling the story of God's activity in creation to this point, and the Service of Light to proclaim the resurrection. There are sometimes baptisms and confirmations and the service usually culminates in Holy Communion. 'Alleluia' rings out and the Paschal Candle, from which all baptism candles for the year will be lit, stands in a prominent position for all to see.

Ascension Day marks the return of Jesus Christ to the Father, and many churches will hold special services or sing from their tower!

Pentecost is the birthday of the Church as the Spirit rests upon the disciples and they are commissioned to proclaim the mission and ministry of Christ to the world.

Trinity Sunday follows, to draw together the essential nature of God as Father, Son and Holy Spirit. Ordinary Time continues as the Church reflects on the rich resources of Scripture and Tradition.

All Saints and **All Souls** are two separate but closely linked days. All Saints' Day gives thanks for all the saints, those we know by their historical deeds and those known only to God, and we celebrate their example and witness. All Souls' Day remembers those departed this life, and often those families who have had funerals during the year will be invited to church for a special service when their loved ones can be remembered by name and commended to God.

Christ the King marks the end of the Church's Year and celebrates Christ reigning in glory as the Lord of all. And then we begin again.

SPIRIT

Time is precious and time is finite. So making good use of time is not only an important lifestyle matter but is also a response to God in faith.

The ordering of the Church's Year enables us to use time well and to consecrate time as an offering of thanksgiving to God. Following the Christian calendar is not just about doing the same things together but is about the common response to God at all times and in all places so that we are changed by the messages contained within the annual cycle of the Church. If we give ourselves to be ruled by God, who is eternal and yet involved in our time here and now, then we are able to discern his will for us more fully and to be ruled not just by desires and the next immediate task but by the law of love and the means of grace. Time can be blessed for God's purposes, and when we hand time back to God, we find we are released from the competing influences around us to know that Christ really does rule in our daily lives as well as in our hearts.

There are some practical things that we can do to follow the spirit of the Church's Year. First, we can commit ourselves to follow this calendar so that our awareness of it seeps into our being and way of life. You can start at any time, not just at Advent. Hear the Gospel stories anew and become part of the rhythm of worship. Be sure to attend on these important days and organize your life around them. Commit yourself especially to participate fully in Holy Week. Be sure to

Prayer Book for Lay People

buy a diary that still has the main religious festivals printed within it. Add the days of the Church's Year, perhaps writing in red ink as these holy days were often referred to as 'red-letter days'.

Common Worship and its supporting material provide many resources to help with worship in the home as well as in church. Each home should have an Advent Wreath, an Advent calendar, certainly a crib and perhaps even an Easter garden.

Gradually, your time is transformed by following the Church's Year, so that you become governed not by the competing demands of the loudest noise but by the sacred nature of time. The word 'holiday' comes from 'holy day'; it is time set aside to celebrate and to be with the Lord. Not every day can be a holiday, but for the Christian, every day can be a holy day.

THE CHURCH'S YEAR

Advent

The First Sunday of Advent
The Second Sunday of Advent
The Third Sunday of Advent
From 17 December (O Sapientia)
   begin the eight days of prayer before Christmas Day
The Fourth Sunday of Advent
Christmas Eve

Christmas

Christmas Day *(25 December)*
The First Sunday of Christmas
The Second Sunday of Christmas

*The days after Christmas Day until the Epiphany traditionally
form a unity of days of special thanksgiving.*

Epiphany

The Epiphany *(6 January)*
The Baptism of Christ (*The First Sunday of Epiphany; the
   Second Sunday of Epiphany when 6 January is a Sunday*)
The Second Sunday of Epiphany
The Third Sunday of Epiphany
The Fourth Sunday of Epiphany
The Presentation of Christ in the Temple
   (Candlemas) *(2 February)*

Ordinary Time

This begins on the day following the Presentation.

The Fifth Sunday before Lent
The Fourth Sunday before Lent
The Third Sunday before Lent
The Second Sunday before Lent
The Sunday next before Lent

Lent

Ash Wednesday
The First Sunday of Lent
The Second Sunday of Lent
The Third Sunday of Lent
The Fourth Sunday of Lent *(Mothering Sunday)*
The Fifth Sunday of Lent *(Passiontide begins)*
Palm Sunday
Monday of Holy Week
Tuesday of Holy Week
Wednesday of Holy Week
Maundy Thursday
Good Friday
Easter Eve

Easter

Easter Day
Monday of Easter Week
Tuesday of Easter Week
Wednesday of Easter Week
Thursday of Easter Week
Friday of Easter Week
Saturday of Easter Week
The Second Sunday of Easter
The Third Sunday of Easter

The Fourth Sunday of Easter
The Fifth Sunday of Easter
The Sixth Sunday of Easter
Ascension Day
From Friday after Ascension Day
begin the nine days of prayer before Pentecost
The Seventh Sunday of Easter *(Sunday after Ascension Day)*
Pentecost (Whit Sunday)

Ordinary Time

This is resumed on the Monday following the Day of
Pentecost
Trinity Sunday
The Thursday after Trinity Sunday may be observed as
The Day of Thanksgiving for the Institution of Holy
Communion (Corpus Christi)
The First Sunday after Trinity
The Second Sunday after Trinity
The Third Sunday after Trinity
The Fourth Sunday after Trinity
The Fifth Sunday after Trinity
The Sixth Sunday after Trinity
The Seventh Sunday after Trinity
The Eighth Sunday after Trinity
The Ninth Sunday after Trinity
The Tenth Sunday after Trinity
The Eleventh Sunday after Trinity
The Twelfth Sunday after Trinity
The Thirteenth Sunday after Trinity
The Fourteenth Sunday after Trinity
The Fifteenth Sunday after Trinity
The Sixteenth Sunday after Trinity
The Seventeenth Sunday after Trinity
The Eighteenth Sunday after Trinity

The Nineteenth Sunday after Trinity
The Twentieth Sunday after Trinity
The Twenty-first Sunday after Trinity
The Last Sunday after Trinity
Dedication Festival *(The First Sunday in October or
    The Last Sunday after Trinity, if date unknown)*
All Saints' Day *(1 November)*
*The Sunday between 30 October and 5 November may be
    kept as All Saints' Sunday or as:*
The Fourth Sunday before Advent
The Third Sunday before Advent
The Second Sunday before Advent
Christ the King *(The Sunday next before Advent)*

HOLY DAYS

The saints and heroes of the faith have long been remembered by Christians of all denominations. In their example, either by a holy life or sacrificial service, we can remember with affection and respect their contribution to the Christian story and rejoice in what God has been able to do with and through them. We remember personal anniversaries and past events, so it is only natural that we should remember those people who have gone before us to inspire us into service, worship and witness.

STRUCTURE

Holy Days or Saints' Days are set throughout the *Common Worship* calendar according to ecumenical tradition. Saints and martyrs are most often remembered on the date of their death. Saints' Days do not usually supplant a Sunday. The Church has a system of observance for its holy ones.

Festivals are important Holy Days that commemorate the 'founding fathers' of the Church. They include the Blessed Virgin Mary, the Apostles and the Evangelists. From the first generation of the Christian experience we remember people and events, such as the Conversion of Paul (25 January), Joseph of Nazareth (19 March), George, Patron of England (23 April), Mary Magdalene (22 July) and the Blessed Virgin Mary (15 August). In the list of Holy Days, Festivals are printed in bold and have full provision of Propers for each day. This provision of *Common Worship* texts includes an Invitation to Confession, a Collect, Gospel Acclamation, Intercession, Introduction to the Peace, Eucharistic Prefaces and Blessing. Many hymn books also have 'office' hymns that have been written for these particular days, and these are regularly used, especially in cathedrals where the daily offering of worship will take full notice of the Church's Holy Days.

Lesser Festivals mark those men and women who have led the way down the centuries since the early Church to today. Collects are provided in *Common Worship* for each of these days, such as Columba (9 June), Richard of Chichester (16 June), and Francis of Assisi (4 October). Further liturgical texts can be used from the material provided from the 'Commons', that is, common or general text of a saint or martyr, a bishop or a teacher, which can be applied to the individual saint. There are exceptions; national saints will be remembered as a festival in their country, such as David

(1 March) in Wales or local saints may be recalled in their special day with great celebration in their locality. So, St Alban (22 June), first martyr of Britain, is remembered as a lesser festival throughout the Church of England but as a Festival by the people of St Alban's Cathedral and Diocese, with great celebration and pilgrimage.

SHAPE

Each Saint's Day, whatever its categorization, will be remembered by a range of readings, prayers, intercessions, special services, liturgical colours or processions according to local tradition and custom. But we all share the saints and their example in the faith. Some books provide a potted history of the work of the saint, and it is good to follow these accounts on each special day. It is also both interesting and helpful to look up what the holy person did for God in a *Lives of the Saints* or a dictionary of the Church, for we can all learn by good example.

Some commemoration is also made of people who have contributed great deeds or sacrifices in more modern times, such as Janani Luwum, Archbishop of Uganda, martyr, 1977, or William Wilberforce, social reformer, 1833. The Church of England does not 'make' or 'canonize' saints but we do remember those who, in our day, have been an inspiration to us all.

SPIRIT

Brother Tristam SSF produced a book called *Exciting Holiness*. This wonderful book encouraged a remembering of the saints and told their stories. When I was asked to contribute information about the little-known St Aldhelm, Bishop of Sherborne (25 May) to whom my parish in Dorset was dedicated, I involved the congregation in determining the biography. We all have our favourite saints and they have a place of affection that stays with us. Saints and holy people are those whose lives have been visibly changed by their relationship with God in Christ – and by remembering and by joining in with their prayers we can hope that our lives may be changed too.

The *Festivals* book (published 2008) is the last of the *Common Worship* texts. The task of writing this book, begun long before 2000, when *Common Worship: Services and Prayers* was first published, has ended nearly a decade later. So the saints come last but not least, and we still remember them, we still learn from them and we still strive with them to do God's will and to transform his world for the good of all.

Since we are surrounded by so great a cloud of witnesses ... let us run with perseverance the race that is set before us, looking to Jesus the pioneer and perfecter of our faith. (Hebrews 12.1, 2)

HOLY DAYS

In the Calendar, Principal Feasts and other Principal Holy Days are printed in **bold**; Festivals and other Sundays are printed in roman typeface. Commemorations are printed in *italics*.

January

1   The Naming and Circumcision of Jesus

2   Basil the Great and Gregory of Nazianzus, bishops, teachers of the faith, 379 and 389

2   Seraphim, monk of Sarov, spiritual guide, 1833

2   Vedanayagam Samuel Azariah, bishop in South India, evangelist, 1945

6   The Epiphany

10   William Laud, Archbishop of Canterbury, 1645

11   Mary Slessor, missionary in West Africa, 1915

12   Aelred of Hexham, Abbot of Rievaulx, 1167

12   Benedict Biscop, Abbot of Wearmouth, scholar, 689

13   Hilary, Bishop of Poitiers, teacher of the faith, 367

13   Kentigern (Mungo), missionary bishop in Strathclyde and Cumbria, 603

13   George Fox, founder of the Society of Friends (the Quakers), 1691

17   Antony of Egypt, hermit, abbot, 356

17   Charles Gore, bishop, founder of the Community of the Resurrection, 1932

18–25   Week of Prayer for Christian Unity

19   Wulfstan, Bishop of Worcester, 1095

20   Richard Rolle of Hampole, spiritual writer, 1349

21   Agnes, child martyr at Rome, 304

22   *Vincent of Saragossa, deacon, first martyr of Spain, 304*

24   Francis de Sales, Bishop of Geneva, teacher of the faith, 1622

25   The Conversion of Paul

26   Timothy and Titus, companions of Paul

28   Thomas Aquinas, priest, philosopher, teacher of the faith, 1274

30   Charles, king and martyr, 1649

31   John Bosco, priest, founder of the Salesian Teaching Order, 1888

February

1   Brigid, Abbess of Kildare, c. 525

2   The Presentation of Christ in the Temple
      (Candlemas)

3   Anskar, Archbishop of Hamburg, missionary in Denmark and Sweden, 865

4   Gilbert of Sempringham, founder of the Gilbertine Order, 1189

6   The Martyrs of Japan, 1597

10   Scholastica, sister of Benedict, Abbess of Plombariola, c. 543

14   Cyril and Methodius, missionaries to the Slavs, 869 and 885

14   Valentine, martyr at Rome, c. 269

15   Sigfrid, bishop, Apostle of Sweden, 1045

15   Thomas Bray, priest, founder of the SPCK and the SPG, 1730

17   Janani Luwum, Archbishop of Uganda, martyr, 1977

23   Polycarp, Bishop of Smyrna, martyr, c. 155

27   George Herbert, priest, poet, 1633

March

1   David, Bishop of Menevia, Patron of Wales, c. 601

2   Chad, Bishop of Lichfield, missionary, 672

7   Perpetua, Felicity and their companions, martyrs at Carthage, 203

8   Edward King, Bishop of Lincoln, 1910

8   Felix, bishop, Apostle to the East Angles, 647

8   Geoffrey Studdert Kennedy, priest, poet, 1929

17   Patrick, bishop, missionary, Patron of Ireland, c. 460

18   Cyril, Bishop of Jerusalem, teacher of the faith, 386
19   Joseph of Nazareth
20   Cuthbert, Bishop of Lindisfarne, missionary, 687
21   Thomas Cranmer, Archbishop of Canterbury,
          Reformation martyr, 1556
24   Walter Hilton of Thurgarton, Augustinian canon, mystic, 1396
24   Oscar Romero, Archbishop of San Salvador, martyr, 1980
**25   The Annunciation of Our Lord to the Blessed Virgin
          Mary**
26   Harriet Monsell, founder of the Community of St John the
          Baptist, 1883
31   John Donne, priest, poet, 1631

April

 1   Frederick Denison Maurice, priest, teacher of the faith, 1872
 9   Dietrich Bonhoeffer, Lutheran pastor, martyr, 1945
10   William Law, priest, spiritual writer, 1761
10   William of Ockham, friar, philosopher, teacher of the faith, 1347
11   George Augustus Selwyn, first Bishop of New Zealand, 1878
16   Isabella Gilmore, deaconess, 1923
19   Alphege, Archbishop of Canterbury, martyr, 1012
21   Anselm, Abbot of Le Bec, Archbishop of Canterbury, teacher
          of the faith, 1109
23   George, martyr, Patron of England, c. 304
24   Mellitus, Bishop of London, first bishop at St Paul's, 624
25   Mark the Evangelist
27   Christina Rossetti, poet, 1894
28   Peter Chanel, missionary in the South Pacific, martyr, 1841
29   Catherine of Siena, teacher of the faith, 1380
30   Pandita Mary Ramabai, translator of the Scriptures, 1922

May

 1   Philip and James, Apostles
 2   Athanasius, Bishop of Alexandria, teacher of the faith, 373

4   English saints and martyrs of the Reformation era

8   Julian of Norwich, spiritual writer, c.1417

14   Matthias the Apostle

16   *Caroline Chisholm, social reformer, 1877*

19   Dunstan, Archbishop of Canterbury, restorer of monastic life, 988

20   Alcuin of York, deacon, Abbot of Tours, 804

21   *Helena, Protector of the Holy Places, 330*

24   John and Charles Wesley, evangelists, hymn writers, 1791 and 1788

25   The Venerable Bede, monk at Jarrow, scholar, historian, 735

25   *Aldhelm, Bishop of Sherborne, 709*

26   Augustine, first Archbishop of Canterbury, 605

26   *John Calvin, reformer, 1564*

26   *Philip Neri, founder of the Oratorians, spiritual guide, 1595*

28   *Lanfranc, Prior of Le Bec, Archbishop of Canterbury, scholar, 1089*

30   Josephine Butler, social reformer, 1906

30   *Joan of Arc, visionary, 1431*

30   *Apolo Kivebulaya, priest, evangelist in Central Africa, 1933*

31   The Visit of the Blessed Virgin Mary to Elizabeth

June

1   Justin, martyr at Rome, c.165

3   *The Martyrs of Uganda, 1885–7 and 1977*

4   *Petroc, Abbot of Padstow, sixth century*

5   Boniface (Wynfrith) of Crediton, bishop, Apostle of Germany, martyr, 754

6   *Ini Kopuria, founder of the Melanesian Brotherhood, 1945*

8   Thomas Ken, Bishop of Bath and Wells, Nonjuror, hymn writer, 1711

9   Columba, Abbot of Iona, missionary, 597

9   *Ephrem of Syria, deacon, hymn writer, teacher of the faith, 373*

11   Barnabas the Apostle

14   *Richard Baxter, Puritan divine, 1691*
15   *Evelyn Underhill, spiritual writer, 1941*
16   Richard, Bishop of Chichester, 1253
16   *Joseph Butler, Bishop of Durham, philosopher, 1752*
17   *Samuel and Henrietta Barnett, social reformers, 1913 and 1936*
18   *Bernard Mizeki, Apostle of the MaShona, martyr, 1896*
19   *Sundar Singh of India, Sadhu (holy man), evangelist, teacher of the faith, 1929*
22   Alban, first martyr of Britain, *c.* 250
23   Etheldreda, Abbess of Ely, *c.* 678
24   The birth of John the Baptist
27   *Cyril, Bishop of Alexandria, teacher of the faith, 444*
28   Irenaeus, Bishop of Lyons, teacher of the faith, *c.* 200
29   Peter and Paul, Apostles

July

1   *Henry, John, and Henry Venn the younger, priests, evangelical divines, 1797, 1813 and 1873*
3   Thomas the Apostle
6   *Thomas More, scholar, and John Fisher, Bishop of Rochester, Reformation martyrs, 1535*
11   Benedict of Nursia, Abbot of Monte Cassino, father of western monasticism, *c.* 550
14   John Keble, priest, Tractarian, poet, 1866
15   Swithun, Bishop of Winchester, *c.* 862
15   *Bonaventure, friar, bishop, teacher of the faith, 1274*
16   *Osmund, Bishop of Salisbury, 1099*
18   *Elizabeth Ferard, first deaconess of the Church of England, founder of the Community of St Andrew, 1883*
19   Gregory, Bishop of Nyssa, and his sister Macrina, deaconess, teachers of the faith, *c.* 394 and *c.* 379
20   *Margaret of Antioch, martyr, fourth century*
20   *Bartolomé de las Casas, Apostle to the Indies, 1566*
22   Mary Magdalene
23   *Bridget of Sweden, Abbess of Vadstena, 1373*

25   James the Apostle
26   Anne and Joachim, parents of the Blessed Virgin Mary
27   *Brooke Foss Westcott, Bishop of Durham, teacher of the*
          faith, 1901
29   Mary, Martha and Lazarus, companions of Our Lord
30   William Wilberforce, social reformer, 1833
31   *Ignatius of Loyola, founder of the Society of Jesus, 1556*

August

4   *Jean-Baptiste Vianney, Curé d'Ars, spiritual guide, 1859*
5   Oswald, King of Northumbria, martyr, 642
6   The Transfiguration of Our Lord
7   *John Mason Neale, priest, hymn writer, 1866*
8   Dominic, priest, founder of the Order of Preachers, 1221
9   Mary Sumner, founder of the Mothers' Union, 1921
10   Laurence, Deacon at Rome, martyr, 258
11   Clare of Assisi, founder of the Minoresses (Poor Clares),
          1253
11   *John Henry Newman, priest, Tractarian, 1890*
13   Jeremy Taylor, Bishop of Down and Connor, teacher of the
          faith, 1667
13   *Florence Nightingale, nurse, social reformer, 1910*
13   *Octavia Hill, social reformer, 1912*
14   *Maximilian Kolbe, friar, martyr, 1941*
15   The Blessed Virgin Mary
20   Bernard, Abbot of Clairvaux, teacher of the faith, 1153
20   *William and Catherine Booth, founders of the Salvation Army,*
          1912 and 1890
24   Bartholomew the Apostle
27   Monica, mother of Augustine of Hippo, 387
28   Augustine, Bishop of Hippo, teacher of the faith, 430
29   The beheading of John the Baptist
30   John Bunyan, spiritual writer, 1688
31   Aidan, Bishop of Lindisfarne, missionary, 651

September

1 *Giles of Provence, hermit, c. 710*
2 *The Martyrs of Papua New Guinea, 1901 and 1942*
3 Gregory the Great, Bishop of Rome, teacher of the faith, 604
4 *Birinus, Bishop of Dorchester (Oxon), Apostle of Wessex, 650*
6 *Allen Gardiner, missionary, founder of the South American Mission Society, 1851*
8 The birth of the Blessed Virgin Mary
9 *Charles Fuge Lowder, priest, 1880*
13 John Chrysostom, Bishop of Constantinople, teacher of the faith, 407
14 Holy Cross Day
15 Cyprian, Bishop of Carthage, martyr, 258
16 Ninian, Bishop of Galloway, Apostle of the Picts, c. 432
16 *Edward Bouverie Pusey, priest, Tractarian, 1882*
17 Hildegard, Abbess of Bingen, visionary, 1179
19 *Theodore of Tarsus, Archbishop of Canterbury, 690*
20 John Coleridge Patteson, first Bishop of Melanesia, and his companions, martyrs, 1871
21 Matthew, Apostle and Evangelist
25 Lancelot Andrewes, Bishop of Winchester, spiritual writer, 1626
25 *Sergei of Radonezh, Russian monastic reformer, teacher of the faith, 1392*
26 *Wilson Carlile, founder of the Church Army, 1942*
27 Vincent de Paul, founder of the Congregation of the Mission (Lazarists), 1660
29 Michael and All Angels
30 *Jerome, translator of the Scriptures, teacher of the faith, 420*

1	*Remigius, Bishop of Rheims, Apostle of the Franks, 533*
1	*Anthony Ashley Cooper, Earl of Shaftesbury, social reformer, 1885*
4	Francis of Assisi, friar, deacon, founder of the Friars Minor, 1226
6	William Tyndale, translator of the Scriptures, Reformation martyr, 1536
9	*Denys, Bishop of Paris, and his companions, martyrs, c. 250*
9	*Robert Grosseteste, Bishop of Lincoln, philosopher, scientist, 1253*
10	Paulinus, Bishop of York, missionary, 644
10	*Thomas Traherne, poet, spiritual writer, 1674*
11	*Ethelburga, Abbess of Barking, 675*
11	*James the Deacon, companion of Paulinus, seventh century*
12	Wilfrid of Ripon, bishop, missionary, 709
12	*Elizabeth Fry, prison reformer, 1845*
12	*Edith Cavell, nurse, 1915*
13	Edward the Confessor, King of England, 1066
15	Teresa of Avila, teacher of the faith, 1582
16	*Nicholas Ridley, Bishop of London, and Hugh Latimer, Bishop of Worcester, Reformation martyrs, 1555*
17	Ignatius, Bishop of Antioch, martyr, c. 107
18	Luke the Evangelist
19	Henry Martyn, translator of the Scriptures, missionary in India and Persia, 1812
25	*Crispin and Crispinian, martyrs at Rome, c. 287*
26	Alfred the Great, King of the West Saxons, scholar, 899
26	*Cedd, Abbot of Lastingham, Bishop of the East Saxons, 664*
28	Simon and Jude, Apostles
29	James Hannington, Bishop of Eastern Equatorial Africa, martyr in Uganda, 1885
31	*Martin Luther, reformer, 1546*

November

1 **All Saints' Day**
2 Commemoration of the Faithful Departed (All Souls' Day)
3 Richard Hooker, priest, Anglican apologist, teacher of the
      faith, 1600
3 Martin of Porres, friar, 1639
6 Leonard, hermit, sixth century
*6 William Temple, Archbishop of Canterbury, teacher of the
      faith, 1944*
7 Willibrord of York, bishop, Apostle of Frisia, 739
8 The Saints and Martyrs of England
9 Margery Kempe, mystic, c. 1440
10 Leo the Great, Bishop of Rome, teacher of the faith, 461
11 Martin, Bishop of Tours, *c.* 397
13 Charles Simeon, priest, evangelical divine, 1836
14 Samuel Seabury, first Anglican bishop in North America, 1796
16 Margaret, Queen of Scotland, philanthropist, reformer of the
      Church, 1093
16 Edmund Rich of Abingdon, Archbishop of Canterbury, 1240
17 Hugh, Bishop of Lincoln, 1200
18 Elizabeth of Hungary, Princess of Thuringia, philanthropist,
      1231
19 Hilda, Abbess of Whitby, 680
19 Mechtild, Béguine of Magdeburg, mystic, 1280
20 Edmund, King of the East Angles, martyr, 870
*20 Priscilla Lydia Sellon, a restorer of the religious life in the Church
      of England, 1876*
22 Cecilia, martyr at Rome, c. 230
23 Clement, Bishop of Rome, martyr, *c.* 100
25 Catherine of Alexandria, martyr, fourth century
25 Isaac Watts, hymn writer, 1748
*29 Day of Intercession and Thanksgiving for the Missionary Work of
      the Church*
30 Andrew the Apostle

December

1	*Charles de Foucauld, hermit in the Sahara, 1916*
3	*Francis Xavier, missionary, Apostle of the Indies, 1552*
4	*John of Damascus, monk, teacher of the faith, c. 749*
4	*Nicholas Ferrar, deacon, founder of the Little Gidding Community, 1637*
6	Nicholas, Bishop of Myra, c. 326
7	Ambrose, Bishop of Milan, teacher of the faith, 397
8	The Conception of the Blessed Virgin Mary
13	Lucy, martyr at Syracuse, 304
13	*Samuel Johnson, moralist, 1784*
14	John of the Cross, poet, teacher of the faith, 1591
17	*O Sapientia*
17	*Eglantyne Jebb, social reformer, founder of 'Save The Children', 1928*
24	Christmas Eve
25	**Christmas Day**
26	Stephen, deacon, first martyr
27	John, Apostle and Evangelist
28	The Holy Innocents
29	Thomas Becket, Archbishop of Canterbury, martyr, 1170
31	*John Wyclif, reformer, 1384*

READINGS FOR THE
MAIN SERVICE ON
SUNDAYS AND FESTIVALS

Sundays are special. Sundays still have a different character from the rest of the week. We would all like a month of Sundays – just once, unless, of course, you work full time for the Church of England, that is! Whether you work on a Sunday or not, we do know that Sunday is the Sabbath for Christians and that it has a unique status. Families meet up for what is often the only meal together during the week, we join in sports and social activities that inspire and renew us, and we worship. Sunday is the Lord's Day and both the beginning and the climax of worship in church each week. Sundays are mini-Easter Days, so we come together to offer our worship as a corporate act and in common ways. Consequently, *Common Worship* provides a lectionary for use on Sundays. A lectionary is a table of carefully chosen readings to be read on set days. The *Common Worship Sunday Lectionary* helps us to discover the Word of God and to reflect upon the riches of Holy Scripture.

STRUCTURE

The *Common Worship Sunday Lectionary* is part of a wider lectionary provision that finds its roots in the *Revised*

Common Lectionary. This is an internationally agreed document that has been adopted by many different denominations, with minor local variations. This means that, in the main, Christians all over the world are listening to and receiving the same biblical readings on each and every Sunday. This has huge significance for preachers and the identity of the Church, which Christ prayed would be 'one'. The *Common Worship Sunday Lectionary* is for the principal service on a Sunday, whether the service is a Eucharist or a Word Service. For each Sunday, provision is made for a reading from the Old Testament, a psalm, a reading from the New Testament, and a Gospel reading. When there are only two readings in a service, the minister has to ensure a balance between the use of the Old Testament and the New Testament. There should always be a Gospel reading.

Each Sunday of the year also has a Collect, a short prayer to be used towards the start of the service, which gathers together the themes of the day, the season and the readings, so that we are praying, literally, in common. Anglican Collects provide a rich vein of prayer and theological understanding and can be a real aid to regular praying. *Common Worship* provides Collects for each and every Sunday and Holy Day in modern language, or traditional language.

SHAPE

The *Common Worship Sunday Lectionary* has a firm shape and pattern that derives from the *Revised Common Lectionary*. The *Sunday Lectionary* works on a three-year cycle, with each of the Synoptic Gospels, Matthew, Mark and Luke, providing the main content. With very few excpetions, the Gospel readings each Sunday follow on from the previous week. This cycle is described as Year A – Matthew; Year B – Mark; and Year C – Luke. Almost the whole of John's Gospel is covered in the three-year cycle. It is read on specific Holy Days, or when the continuous reading of a Gospel may be changed for the season, for example, in Advent or Lent. The Old and New Testament readings are related to the Gospel reading of the day, and this enables the listener to become immersed not just in Scripture as a whole but also in the style, perspective and message of the Gospel author.

Each lectionary year begins on Advent Sunday. So Year A – Matthew is 2007/8; Year B – Mark is 2008/9; Year C – Luke 2009/10; and so on. See page 105.

The Old and New Testament passages are often read in church by lay people. These readers should be chosen from all ages and groups within the congregation, the only qualification being that they should be able to read aloud well. The Gospel is most regularly read by a deacon or the presiding minister, often from a prominent position or, following a procession, from among the body of the people. It is customary to stand for the reading of the Gospel.

SPIRIT

Reading Scripture in common and with an organized pattern such as a lectionary is an effective way of hearing Scripture and an effective sign of unity. Through common themes and regular patterns of prayer, Anglicans can make Sundays their own and ensure that Sunday worship sets the tone for the week.

Preparing for Sunday worship is important. Preachers have the habit of reading the Scripture passages for the coming Sunday early on in the week. If I am preaching on a Sunday, I read the coming readings first thing on the preceding Monday morning. This means that the mind can mull over the text and draw on real-life experiences, along with study and reflection, so that the sermon comes more easily towards the end of the week.

This kind of preparation is good practice for all Christians. If your parish has a weekly notice sheet or a monthly magazine, the forthcoming readings can be reproduced so that people can prepare for the reading and the preaching that they will soon hear. It is a long-standing but under-used tradition in the Church of England to read the lessons for Sunday before coming to church. A list of the readings is on pages 105–14 of this book, and a copy of the lectionary with readings printed out can also be purchased in inexpensive form.

Following a lectionary can also encourage greater study and reflection. Clergy and others will be able to help with suggesting Bible reading notes or biblical commentaries. Parishes may well have Bible study groups or home groups so that the forthcoming readings for a Sunday or even a Season can be studied.

Holy Scripture is a dynamic provision of meaningful passages of power. The more we plan, prepare and reflect upon the readings on Sundays, and indeed every day, the more we listen to God and find strength in his revelation.

READINGS FOR THE MAIN SERVICE ON SUNDAYS AND FESTIVALS

For dates of Years A, B and C see page 209.
Please note that if a Principal Feast falls or a Festival is celebrated on a Sunday in a particular year, the readings for that occasion replace the Sunday readings given here.

Day	Year A	Year B	Year C
Advent 1	Isa. 2.1–5 Rom. 13.11–14 Matt. 24.36–44	Isa. 64.1–9 I Cor. 1.3–9 Mk 13.24–37	Jer. 33.14–16 I Thess. 3.9–13 Lk. 21.25–36
Advent 2	Isa. 11.1–10 Rom. 15.4–13 Matt. 3.1–12	Isa. 40.1–11 2 Pet. 3.8–15a Mk 1.1–8	Bar. 5.1–9 or Mal. 3.1–4 Phil. 1.3–11 Lk. 3.1–6
Advent 3	Isa. 35.1–10 James 5.7–10 Matt. 11.2–11	Isa. 61.1–4, 8–11 I Thess. 5.16–24 Jn 1.6–8, 19–28	Zeph. 3.14–20 Phil. 4.4–7 Lk. 3.7–18
Advent 4	Isa. 7.10–16 Rom. 1.1–7 Matt. 1.18–25	2 Sam. 7.1–11, 16 Rom. 16.25–27 Lk. 1.26–38	Micah 5.2–5a Heb. 10.5–10 Lk. 1.39–45(46–55)
Christmas set 1	Isa. 9.2–7 Tit. 2.11–14 Lk. 2.1–14(15–20)	See A	See A
Christmas set 2	Isa. 62.6–12 Tit. 3.4–7 Lk. 2.(1–7)8–20	See A	See A
Christmas set 3	Isa. 52.7–10 Heb. 1.1–4(5–12) Jn 1.1–14	See A	See A

Day	Year A	Year B	Year C
Christmas 1	Isa. 63.7–9 Heb. 2.10–18 Matt. 2.13–23	Isa. 61.10 – 62.3 Gal. 4.4–7 Lk. 2.15–21	1 Sam. 2.18–20, 26 Col. 3.12–17 Lk. 2.41–52
Christmas 2	Jer. 31.7–14 or Eccl. 24.1–12 Eph. 1.3–14 Jn 1. (1–9)10–18	See A	See A
Epiphany	Isa. 60.1–6 Eph. 3.1–12 Matt. 2.1–12	See A	See A
Baptism of Christ	Isa. 42.1–9 Acts 10.34–43 Matt. 3.13–17	Gen. 1.1–5 Acts 19.1–7 Mk 1.4–11	Isa. 43.1–7 Acts 8.14–17 Lk. 3.15–17, 21–22
Epiphany 2	Isa. 49.1–7 1 Cor. 1.1–9 Jn 1.29–42	1 Sam. 3.1–10 (11–20) Rev. 5.1–10 Jn 1.43–51	Isa. 62.1–5 1 Cor. 12.1–11 Jn 2.1–11
Epiphany 3	Isa. 9.1–4 1 Cor. 1.10–18 Matt. 4.12–23	Gen. 14.17–20 Rev. 19.6–10 Jn 2.1–11	Neh. 8.1–3, 5–6, 8–10 1 Cor. 12.12–31a Lk. 4.14–21
Epiphany 4	1 Kgs 17.8–16 1 Cor. 1.8–31 Jn 2.1–11	Deut. 18.15–20 Rev. 12.1–5a Mk 1.21–28	Ezek. 43.27 – 44.4 1 Cor. 13.1–13 Lk. 2.22–40
Presentation	Mal. 3.1–5 Heb. 2.14–18 Lk. 2.22–40	See A	See A
4–10 February	Isa. 58.1–9a(9b–12) 1 Cor. 2.1–12(13–16) Matt. 5.13–20	Isa. 40.21–31 1 Cor. 9.16–23 Mk 1. 29–39	Isa. 6.1–8(9–13) 1 Cor. 15.1–11 Lk. 5.1–11
11–17 February	Deut. 30.15–20 or Ecclus. 15.15–20 1 Cor. 3.1–9 Matt. 5.21–37	2 Kgs 5.1–14 1 Cor. 9.24–27 Mk 1.40–45	Jer. 17.5–10 1 Cor. 15.12–20 Lk. 6.17–26

Day	Year A	Year B	Year C
18–24 February	Lev. 19.1–2, 9–18 1 Cor. 3.10–11, 16–23 Matt. 5.38–48	Isa. 43.18–25 2 Cor. 1.18–22 Mk 2.1–12	Gen. 45.3–11, 15 1 Cor. 15.35–38, 42–50 Lk. 6.27–38
2 before Lent	Gen. 1.1 – 2.3 Rom. 8.18–25 Matt. 6.25–34	Prov. 8.1, 22–31 Col. 1.15–20 Jn 1.1–14	Gen. 2.4b–9, 15–25 Rev. 4 Lk. 8.22–25
Next before Lent	Ex. 24.12–18 2 Pet. 1.16–21 Matt. 17.1–9	2 Kgs 2.1–12 2 Cor. 4.3–6 Mk 9.2–9	Ex. 34.29–35 2 Cor. 3.12 – 4.2 Lk. 9.28b–36, (37–43a)
Ash Wednesday	Joel 2.1–2, 12–17 or Isa. 58.1–12 2 Cor. 5.20b – 6.10 Matt. 6.1–6, 16–21 or Jn 8.1–11	See A	See A
Lent 1	Gen. 2.15–17; 3.1–7 Rom. 5.12–19 Matt. 4.1–11	Gen. 9.8–17 1 Pet. 3.18–22 Mk 1.9–15	Deut. 26.1–11 Rom. 10.8b–13 Lk 4.1–13
Lent 2	Gen. 12.1–4a Rom. 4.1–5, 13–17 Jn 3.1–17	Gen. 17.1–7, 15–16 Rom. 4.13–25 Mk 8.31–38	Gen. 15.1–12, 17–18 Phil. 3.17 – 4.1 Lk.13.31–35
Lent 3	Ex. 17.1–7 Rom. 5.1–11 Jn 4.5–42	Ex. 20.1–17 1 Cor. 1.18–25 Jn 2.13–22	Isa. 55.1–9 1 Cor. 10.1–13 Lk. 13.1–9
Lent 4	1 Sam. 16.1–13 Eph. 5.8–14 Jn 9.1–41	Num. 21.4–9 Eph. 2.1–10 Jn 3.14–21	Josh. 5.9–12 2 Cor. 5.16–21 Lk. 15.1–3,11b–32
Mothering Sunday	Ex. 2.1–10 or 1 Sam. 1.20–28 2 Cor. 1.3–7 or Col. 3.12–17 Lk. 2.33–35 or Jn 19.25–27	See A	See A

Day	Year A	Year B	Year C
Lent 5	Ezek. 37.1–14 Rom. 8. 6–11 Jn 11.1–45	Jer. 31.31–34 Heb. 5.5–10 Jn 12.20–33	Isa. 43.16–21 Phil. 3.4b–14 Jn 12.1–8
Palm Sunday	Isa. 50.4–9a Phil. 2.5–11 Matt. 26.14 – 27.66 or 27.11–54	Isa. 50.4–9a Phil. 2.5–11 Mk 14.1 – 15.47 or 15.1–19(40–47)	Isa. 50.4–9a Phil. 2.5–11 Lk. 22.14 – 23.56 or 23.1–49
Maundy Thursday	Ex. 12.1–4(5–10) 11–14 I Cor. 11. 23–26 Jn 13.1–17, 31b–35	See A	See A
Good Friday	Isa. 52.13 – 53.12 Heb. 10.16–25 or Heb. 4.14–16; 5.7–9 Jn 18.1 – 19.42	See A	See A
Easter*	Acts 10.34–43 or Jer. 31.1–6 Col. 3.1–4 Jn 20.1–18 or Matt. 28.1–10	Acts 10.34–43 or Isa. 25.6–9 I Cor. 15.1–11 Jn 20.1–18 or Mk 16.1–8	Acts 10.34–43 or Isa. 65.17–25 I Cor. 15.19–26 Jn 20.1–18 or Lk. 24.1–12
Easter 2*	Ex. 14.10–31; 15.20–21 or Acts 2.14a, 22–32 I Pet. 1.3–9 Jn 20.19–31	Acts 4.32–35 I Jn 1.1 – 2.2 Jn 20.19–31	Acts 5.27–32 Rev. 1.4–8 Jn 20.19–31
Easter 3*	Zeph. 3.14–20 or Acts 2.14a, 36–41 I Pet. 1.17–23 Lk. 24.13–35	Acts 3.12–19 I Jn 3.1–7 Lk. 24.36b–48	Acts 9.1–6(7–20) Rev. 5.11–14 Jn 21.1–19
Easter 4*	Gen. 7 or Acts 2.42–47 I Pet. 2.19–25 Jn 10.1–10	Gen. 7.1–5, 11–18; 9.8–14 or Acts 4.5–12 I Jn 3.16–24 Jn 10.11–18	Acts 9.36–43 Rev. 7.9–17 Jn 10.22–30

*The readings from Acts must be used as either the first or second reading.

Day	Year A	Year B	Year C
Easter 5*	Gen. 8.1–19 or Acts 7.55–60	Baruch 3.9–15, 32–36; 4.1–4 or Gen. 22.1–18 or Acts 8.26–40	Acts 11.1–18
	I Pet. 2.2–10	I Jn 4.7–21	Rev. 21.1–6
	Jn 14.1–14	Jn 15.1–8	Jn 13.31–35
Easter 6*	Gen. 8.20–9.17 or Acts 17.22–31	Isa. 55.1–11 or Acts 10.44–48	Acts 16.9–15
	I Pet. 3.13–22	I Jn 5.1–6	Rev. 21.10, 22 – 22.5
	Jn 14.15–21	Jn 15.9–17	Jn 14.23–29
Ascension Day	Dan. 7.9–14 or Acts 1.1–11 Eph. 1.15–23 Lk. 24.44–53	See A	See A
Easter 7*	Ezek. 36.24–28 or Acts 1.6–14	Acts 1.15–17, 21–26	Acts 16.16–34
	I Pet. 4.12–14; 5.6–11	I Jn 5.9–13	Rev. 22.12–14, 16–17, 20–21
	Jn 17.1–11	Jn 17.6–19	Jn 17. 20–26
Pentecost	Acts 2.1–21 or Num. 11.24–30 I Cor. 12.3b–13	Acts 2.1–21 or Ezek. 37.1–14 Rom. 8.22–27	Acts 2. 1–21 or Gen. 11.1–9 Rom. 8.14–17 or Acts 2.1–21
	Jn 20.19–23 or Jn 7.37–39	Jn 15.26–27; 16.4b–15	Jn 14.8–17, (25–27)
Trinity Sunday	Gen. 1.1–2.4a or Isa. 40.12–17, 27–31 2 Cor. 13.11–13 Matt. 28.16–20	Isa. 6.1–8 Rom. 8.12–17 Jn 3.1–17	Prov. 8.1–4, 22–31 Rom. 5.1–5 John 16.12–15
Corpus Christi	Gen. 14.18–20 I Cor. 11. 23–26 Jn 6.51–58	See A	See A

Day	Year A	Year B	Year C
24–28 May	See 18–24 February readings, depending on the date of Easter.		
29 May–4 June	Gen. 6.9–22; 7.24 8.14–19 or Deut. 11.18–21, 26–28 Rom. 1.16–17; 3.22b–28(29–31) Matt. 7.21–29	I Sam. 3.1–10, (11–20) or Deut. 5.12–15 2 Cor. 4.5–12 Mk 2.23 – 3.6	I Kgs 18.20–21 (22–29)30–39 or I Kgs 8. 22–23, 41–43 Gal. 1.1–12 Lk. 7.1–10
5–11 June	Gen. 12.1–9 or Hos. 5.15 – 6.6 Rom. 4.13–25 Matt. 9.9–13, 18–26	I Sam. 8.4–11(12–15) 16–20(11.14–15) or Gen. 3.8–15 2 Cor. 4.13 – 5.1 Mk 3.20–35	I Kgs 17.8–16 (17–24) or I Kgs 17.17–24 Gal. 1.11–24 Lk. 7.11–17
12–18 June	Gen. 18.1–15; (21.1–7) or Ex. 19.2–8a Rom. 5.1–8 Matt. 9.35 – 10.8(9–23)	I Sam. 15.34 – 16.3 or Ezek. 17.22–24 2 Cor. 5.6–10 (11–13), 14–17 Mk 4.26–34	I Kgs 21.1–10(11–14) 15–21a or 2 Sam. 11.26 – 12.10, 13–15 Gal. 2.15–21 Lk. 7.36 – 8.3
19–25 June	Gen. 21.8–21 or Jer. 20.7–13 Rom. 6.1b–11 Matt. 10.24–39	I Sam. 17.(1a, 4–11, 19–23)32–49 or I Sam. 17.57 – 18.5, 10–16 or Job 38.1–11 2 Cor. 6.1–13 Mk 4.35–41	I Kgs 19.1–4, (5–7), 8–15a or Isa. 65.1–9 Gal. 3.23–29 Lk. 8.26–39
26 June–2 July	Gen. 22.1–14 or Jer. 28.5–9 Rom. 6.12–23 Matt. 10.40–42	2 Sam. 1.1, 17–27 or Wisd. Sol. 1.13–15; 2.23–24 2 Cor. 8.7–15 Mk 5.21–43	2 Kgs 2.1–2, 6–14 or I Kgs 19.5–16, 19–21 Gal. 5.1, 13–25 Lk. 9.51–62

Day	Year A	Year B	Year C
3–9 July	Gen. 24.34–38, 42–49, 58–67	2 Sam. 5.1–5, 9–10	2 Kgs 5.1–14
	or Zech. 9.9–12	or Ezek. 2.1–5	Isa. 66.10–14
	Rom. 7.15–25a	2 Cor. 12.2–10	Gal. 6.(1–6)7–16
	Matt. 11.16–19, 25–30	Mk 6.1–13	Lk. 10.1–11, 16–20
10–16 July	Gen. 25.19–34	2 Sam. 6.1–5, 12b–19	Amos 7.7–17
	or Isa. 55.10–13	or Amos 7.7–15	or Deut. 30. 9–14
	Rom. 8.1–11	Eph. 1.3–14	Col. 1.1–14
	Matt. 13.1–9, 18–23	Mk 6.14–29	Lk. 10.25–37
17–23 July	Gen. 28.10–19a	2 Sam. 7.1–14a	Amos 8.1–12
	or Wisd. Sol. 12.13, 16–19	or Jer. 23.1–6	or Gen. 18. 1–10a
	Rom. 8.12–25	Eph. 2.11–22	Col. 1.15–28
	Matt. 13.24–30, 36–43	Mk 6.30–34, 53–56	Lk. 10.38–42
24–30 July	Gen. 29.15–28	2 Sam. 11.1–15	Hos. 1.2–10
	or 1 Kgs 3.5–12	or 2 Kgs 4.42–44	or Gen. 18.20–32
	Rom. 8.26–39	Eph. 3.14–21	Col. 2.6–15(16–19)
	Matt. 13.31–33, 44–52	Jn 6 1–21	Lk. 11.1–13
31 July– 6 August	Gen. 32.22–31	2 Sam. 11.26 – 12.13a	Hos. 11.1–11
	or Isa. 55.1–5	or Ex. 16.2–4, 9–15	or Eccles. 1.2, 12–14; 2.18–23
	Rom. 9.1–5	Eph. 4.1–16	Col. 3.1–11
	Matt. 14.13–21	Jn 6.24–35	Lk. 12.13–21
7–13 August	Gen. 37.1–4, 12–28	2 Sam. 18.5–9, 15, 31–33	Isa. 1.1, 10–20
	or 1 Kgs 19.9–18	or 1 Kgs 19.4–8	or Gen. 15.1–6
	Rom. 10.5–15	Eph. 4.25 – 5.2	Heb. 11.1–3, 8–16
	Matt. 14.22–33	Jn 6.35, 41–51	Lk. 12.32–40
14–20 August	Gen. 45.1–15	1 Kgs 2.10–12; 3.3–14	Isa. 5.1–7
	or Isa. 56.1, 6–8	or Prov. 9.1–6	or Jer. 23. 23–29
	Rom. 11.1–2a, 29–32	Eph. 5.15–20	Heb. 11.29 – 12.2
	Matt. 15.(10–20)21–28	Jn 6.51–58	Lk. 12.49–56

Day	Year A	Year B	Year C
21–27 August	Ex. 1.8 – 2.10	1 Kgs 8. (1, 6, 10–11) 22–30, 41–43	Jer. 1.4–10
	or Isa. 51.1–6	or Josh. 24.1–2a, 14–18	or Isa. 58. 9b–14
	Rom. 12.1–8	Eph. 6.10–20	Heb. 12.18–29
	Matt. 16.13–20	Jn 6.56–69	Lk. 13.10–17
28 August– 3 September	Ex. 3.1–15 or Jer. 15.15–21	S. of S. 2.8–13 or Deut. 4.1–2, 6–9	Jer. 2.4–13 or Ecclus. 10.12–18 or Prov. 25.6–7
	Rom. 12.9–21	James 1.17–27	Heb. 13.1–8, 15–16
	Matt. 16.21–28	Mk 7.1–8, 14–15, 21–23	Lk. 14.1, 7–14
4–10 September	Ex. 12.1–14	Prov. 22.1–2, 8–9, 22–23	Jer. 18.1–11
	or Ezek. 33.7–11	or Isa. 35.4–7a	or Deut. 30.15–20
	Rom. 13.8–14	James 2.1–10 (11–13) 14–17	Philemon 1–21
	Matt. 18.15–20	Mk 7.24–37	Lk. 14.25–33
11–17 September	Ex. 14.19–31 or Ex. 15.1b–11, 21	Prov. 1.20–33	Jer. 4.11–12, 22–28
	or Gen. 50.15–21	or Wisd. Sol. 7.26 – 8.1 or Isa. 50.4–9a	or Ex. 32.7–14
	Rom. 14.1–12	James 3.1–12	1 Tim. 1.12–17
	Matt. 18.21–35	Mk 8.27–38	Lk. 15.1–10
18–24 September	Ex. 16.2–15 or Jonah 3.10 – 4.11	Prov. 31.10–31 or Wisd. Sol. 1.16 – 2.1, 12–22 or Jer. 11.18–20	Jer. 8.18 – 9.1 or Amos 8.4–7
	Phil. 1.21–30	James 3.13 – 4.3, 7–8a	1 Tim. 2.1–7
	Matt. 20.1–16	Mk 9.30–37	Lk. 16.1–13
25 Sept.– 1 October	Ex. 17.1–7	Esth. 7.1–6, 9–10; 9.20–22	Jer. 32.1–3a, 6–15
	or Ezek. 18.1–4, 25–32	or Num. 11.4–6, 10–16, 24–29	or Amos 6.1a, 4–7

Day	Year A	Year B	Year C
	Phil. 2.1–13	James 5.13–20	1 Tim. 6. 6–19
	Matt. 21.23–32	Mk 9.38–50	Lk. 16.19–31
2–8 October	Ex. 20.1–4, 7–9, 12–20 or Isa. 5.1–7 Phil. 3. 4b–14 Matt. 21.33–46	Job 1.1; 2.1–10 or Gen. 2.18–24 Heb. 1.1–4; 2.5–12 Mk 10.2–16	Lament. 1.1–6 or Hab. 1.1–4; 2.1–4 2 Tim. 1.1–14 Lk. 17. 5–10
9–15 October	Ex. 32.1–14 or Isa. 25.1–9 Phil. 4.1–9 Matt. 22.1–14	Job 23.1–9, 16–17 or Amos 5.6–7, 10–15 Heb. 4.12–16 Mk 10.17–31	Jer. 29.1, 4–7 or 2 Kgs 5.1–3, 7–15c 2 Tim. 2. 8–15 Lk. 17.11–19
16–22 October	Ex. 33.12–23 or Isa. 45.1–7 1 Thess. 1.1–10 Matt. 22.15–22	Job 38.1–7(34–41) or Isa. 53.4–12 Heb. 5.1–10 Mk 10.35–45	Jer. 31.27–34 or Gen. 32. 22–31 2 Tim. 3.14 – 4.5 Lk. 18.1–8
23–29 October	Deut. 34.1–12 or Lev. 19.1–2, 15–18 1 Thess. 2.1–8 Matt. 22.34–46	Job 42.1–6,10–17 or Jer. 31.7–9 Heb. 7.23–28 Mk 10.46–52	Joel 2.23–32 or Eccl. 35.12–17 or Jer. 14. 7–10, 19–22 2 Tim. 4. 6–8, 16–18 Lk. 18.9–14
Bible	Neh. 8.1–4a(5–6) 8–12 Col. 3.12–17 Matt. 24.30–35	Isa. 55.1–11 2 Tim. 3.14 – 4.5 Jn 5.36b–47	Isa. 45.22–25 Rom. 15.1–6 Lk. 4.16–24
Dedication	1 Kgs 8.22–30 or Rev. 21.9–14 Heb. 12.18–24 Matt. 21.12–16	Gen. 28.11–18 or Rev. 21.9–14 1 Pet. 2.1–10 Jn 10.22–29	1 Chron. 29.6–19 Eph. 2.19–22 Jn 2. 13–22
4 before Advent	Micah 3.5–12 1 Thess. 2.9–13 Matt. 24.1–14	Deut. 6.1–9 Heb. 9.11–14 Mk 12.28–34	Isa. 1.10–18 2 Thess. 1.1–12 Lk. 19.1–10

Day	Year A	Year B	Year C
All Saints'	Rev. 7.9–17	Wisd. Sol. 3.1–9 or Isa. 25.6–9	Dan. 7.1–3, 15–18
	1 Jn 3.1–3	Rev. 21.1–6a	Eph. 1.11–23
	Matt. 5.1–12	Jn 11.32–44	Lk. 6.20–31
3 before Advent	Wisd. Sol. 6.12–16 or Wisd. Sol. 6.17–20 or Amos 5.18–24	Jonah 3.1–5, 10	Job 19.23–27a
	1 Thess. 4.13–18	Heb. 9.24–28	2 Thess. 2.1–5, 13–17
	Matt. 25.1–13	Mk 1.14–20	Lk. 20.27–38
2 before Advent	Zeph. 1.7, 12–18	Dan. 12.1–3	Mal. 4.1–2a
	1 Thess. 5.1–11	Heb. 10.11–14 (15–18)19–25	2 Thess. 3.6–13
	Matt. 25.14–30	Mk 13.1–8	Lk. 21.5–19
Christ the King	Ezek. 34.11–16, 20–24	Dan. 7.9–10, 13–14	Jer. 23.1–6
	Eph. 1.15–23	Rev. 1.4b–8	Col. 1.11–20
	Matt. 25.31–46	Jn 18. 33–37	Lk. 23.33–43

THE RECONCILIATION
OF A PENITENT

Do not read any further if you want to persist with any preconceptions about this ministry. Prejudice, situation comedy and farce all have their place, but no place in this most misunderstood yet really valuable of liturgical ministries of the Church. *Common Worship* provides liturgy for an aspect of Anglican ministry that has been quietly used for centuries, yet, because of its very nature, has often been ignored. The Book of Common Prayer contains this pastoral exhortation:

> . . . if there be any of you, who by this means [self-examination, confession and repentance] cannot quiet his own conscience herein, but requireth further comfort or counsel, let him come to me, or to some other discreet and learned Minister of God's Word, and open his grief; that by the ministry of God's holy Word he may receive the benefit of absolution, together with ghostly counsel and advice, to the quieting of his conscience, and avoiding of all scruple and doubtfulness.

Sin is bad for you. Confession of sin and receiving absolution is good for you.

Reconciliation is therefore to be used when:

- a person's conscience is burdened by sin or guilt;
- a person wishes to make a new beginning in the Christian life;
- reconciliation is part of a personal, regular discipline.

This ministry can be informal or formal, depending on the pastoral situation. It may be exercised on your own, or, more likely, in the company of an experienced priest, or at a corporate service of penitence when a group or a community need to come before God in sorrow. God's forgiveness is the same; it's just the context that changes to be more or less personal. The text provided here is for use with a penitent and a priest and is to be seen in the wider context of recovering our baptismal status after, well, 'mucking things up', as we so often do by our deliberate action, or omission, or just indifference.

STRUCTURE

This liturgy is a personal moment, with the priest acting on behalf of the Church and God listening in. It is a time of reflection, and what is happening is best described by the title 'reconciliation' as opposed to the historic short-hand of 'confession', which concentrates solely on the role of the penitent. The rubric encourages a time of private preparation before meeting the priest. The priest is responsible for ensuring that the penitent knows what to do, what to expect and how to make 'confession' in whichever way they have agreed.

The titles of each section of the liturgy describe well

the nature of this important short service: The Gathering, The Liturgy of the Word, Confession and Counsel, Reconciliation, Thanksgiving, Dismissal. After gathering, words of Scripture are said and the priest and penitent pray together using the words of Psalm 51. The Confession is made using the framework provided, so that there is a way to begin and a way to end whatever the penitent wishes to say. This may be said from memory or from notes (these notes should be destroyed by the priest after the service). The priest may give appropriate counsel and a penance. The next key component is an act of contrition, which is immediately followed by absolution. God's forgiveness follows instantly from our return to him. The Dismissal is made, ending with perhaps some of the most powerful words in Christian ministry as the priest concludes with: 'Go in peace, and pray for me, a sinner.'

SHAPE

The way in which this service of restoration is celebrated will vary according to tradition and need. Some may need such a formal, clear, objective moment in time to feel assured of God's forgiveness and a new beginning. Others may value a more informal method with spiritual direction and confession combining in a conversational way and absolution concluding such a time together. This liturgy need not necessarily take place in church. Whatever the way in which the penitent is reconciled with God, it is important that careful teaching, explanation and preparation is made of the penitent by the priest before the liturgy begins. The starting point for the priest is a generous spirit. The priest will seek to bring release to the penitent by helping with advice about the corrosive nature of guilt and the opportunity for release. Every priest is bound by the strict, rigid and trustworthy promise of confidentiality.

SPIRIT

Sin affects the whole Church. We regularly confess our sins with general words when we come to church. But sometimes we need to come before God as individuals, and to be specific, just as, when we need to make a sincere apology to someone, we must do that personally – if possible, face to face. The priest is simply exercising the ministry of forgiveness given to the Church by Jesus Christ. How often this ministry takes place will depend on personal discipline and local practice. Jesus will have given God's forgiveness many more times throughout his ministry than simply those occasions recorded in the Gospels.

This ministry takes place far more often than many faithful Christians realize. It is a ministry that is powerful, necessary and, sometimes, all that is left. We all need to examine our own consciences from time to time, and to ask God, through our contrition, to amend our lives. His forgiveness is one of his greatest gifts. As to who should make use of this ministry, and whether it is for you . . . well, here is a traditional Anglican understanding of the ministry of reconciliation.

All may. None must. Some should. Think about it.

THE RECONCILIATION OF A PENITENT

The Gathering

Be still for a while and place yourself in the presence of God.
When you are ready, come and kneel or sit with the priest, who
may welcome you with these or other suitable words.

The Greeting

In the name of the Father,
and of the Son,
and of the Holy Spirit.
Amen.

The Lord Jesus Christ, who came to reconcile sinners,
welcomes all who are penitent.
Grace, mercy and peace be with you.
And also with you.

The Liturgy of the Word

Readings

The priest may say:

The Lord our God is gracious and merciful; he does not desire the death of sinners but rather that they should turn from their sins and live. He has given power and commandment to his ministers, to declare and pronounce to his penitent people the absolution and remission of their sins. He pardons and absolves all those who truly repent and believe in his holy gospel. Let us therefore pray that he will grant you true repentance and the grace and confort of the Holy Spirit.

or

If we say we have no sin, we deceive ourselves, and the truth is not in us. If we confess our sins, God is faithful and just to forgive us our sins and to cleanse us from all unrighteousness. (1 John 1.8, 9)

The priest and penitent say together:

Have mercy on me, O God, in your great goodness;
according to the abundance of your compassion
   blot out my offences.
Wash me thoroughly from my wickedness
and cleanse me from my sin.
Make me a clean heart, O God,
and renew a right spirit within me. (Psalm 51.1, 2, 11)

Other suitable verses from Scripture may be said:

Matthew 6.14, 15; Matthew 11.28; Mark 1.14, 15; Luke 6.31–38; Luke 15. 1–7; John 3.16; John 10.19–23; Romans 5.6–9; 8.1–2; Romans 8.38, 39; Ephesians 5.1, 2; Colossians 1.12–14; Colossians 3.8–10, 12–17; 1 Timothy 1.15; 1 John 1.6, 7, 9; 2.1, 2.

Confession and Counsel

The priest says:

The Lord be in your heart and on your lips
that you may truly and humbly confess your sins.

Confession

Now confess in your own words, beginning:

I confess to almighty God,
before the whole company of heaven and before you ...

or

Almighty God,
long-suffering and of great goodness:
I confess to you,
I confess with my whole heart
my neglect and forgetfulness of your commandments,
my wrong doing, thinking, and speaking;
the hurts I have done to others,
and the good I have left undone.
In particular I confess [since my last confession in . . ./
in this my first confession] ...

O God, for these, and all other sins that I cannot now remember,
I ask your forgiveness.
Forgive me, for I have sinned against you;
and raise me to newness of life;
through Jesus Christ our Lord.
Amen.

The priest may give appropriate counsel or guidance and
whatever help is necessary to enable you to complete your confession.
The priest will encourage you to make restitution, and may
recommend some prayer or action as a sign of repentance.

Reconciliation

Act of Contrition

Make an act of contrition using these, or your own, words:

My God, for love of you
I desire to hate and forsake all sins
by which I have ever displeased you;
and I resolve by the help of your grace
to commit them no more;
and to avoid all opportunities of sin.
Help me to do this,
through Jesus Christ our Lord.
Amen.

Absolution

The priest lays hands on you or extends hands over you.
The priest may make the sign of the cross over you or on your
forehead. The priest says an absolution, such as:

Our Lord Jesus Christ,
who has left power to his Church to absolve all sinners
    who truly repent and believe in him,
of his great mercy forgive you your offences:
and by his authority committed to me,
I absolve you from all your sins,

in the name of the Father,
and of the Son, and of the Holy Spirit.
Amen.

or

God, the Father of all mercies,
has reconciled the world to himself
through the death and resurrection of his Son, Jesus Christ,
not counting our trespasses against us,
but sending his Holy Spirit
to shed abroad his love among us.
By the ministry of reconciliation
entrusted by Christ to his Church,
receive his pardon and peace
to stand before him in his strength alone,
this day and evermore.
Amen.

Thanksgiving

The priest may invite you to give thanks:

Give thanks to the Lord, for he is gracious,
for his faithfulness endures for ever.
For as the heavens are high above the earth,
so great is his mercy upon those who fear him.
As far as the east is from the west,
so far has he set our sins from us.
(Psalm 106.1; 103.11, 12)

God of grace and life,
in your love you have given us a place among your people;
keep us faithful to our baptism,

and prepare us for that glorious day
when the whole creation will be made perfect
in your Son, our Saviour Jesus Christ.
Amen.

The Lord's Prayer

The Lord's Prayer may be said.

The Dismissal

May Christ,
who out of defeat brings new hope and a new future,
fill you with his new life;
and the blessing of God almighty,
the Father, the Son, and the Holy Spirit,
be upon you and remain with you always.
Amen.

The Dismissal

Priest   The Lord has put away your sins.
Penitent **Thanks be to God.**

Priest   Go in peace, and pray for me, a sinner.

HOLY BAPTISM WITHIN A CELEBRATION OF HOLY COMMUNION

The Bishop came to church one Sunday. There was a baptism in the Eucharist. The Bishop preached about the importance of baptism for us all, and presided over the Eucharist. As parish priest I baptized the baby, having nurtured the young family, who came slightly anxiously with their friends that Sunday. At the end of the service, the Bishop asked for the babe, and taking her in his arms, carried her round the church showing her to all the people. The final hymn was not long enough for him to get all round the church, so he proclaimed that we should sing it again, and so we did. Everybody felt that they had joined in this wonderful sacrament of membership. The family, somewhat taken aback, nevertheless felt special and that 'something' had happened to them.

For all of the fuss of having the Bishop visit, the most important person that Sunday was the baby being baptized. And by showing us all how important this moment was for this child, the Bishop reminded us just how important this sacrament is for us all and for our Christian life. The family became regular churchgoers, the baby's grandad was later confirmed and is now the churchwarden. The Lord has added to our number.

STRUCTURE

Baptism is celebrated in many different ways and at different times. A private baptism may take place, or there may be a special service of baptism, but by far the best form of baptism is as part of the main Sunday service within the context of the Eucharist. The Lord's family must be there to welcome its newest members, and the Lord's family must make it a high priority to be welcoming and to be aware of how much renewal a baptism can bring to the community of faith. If baptism is how we come to belong both to Christ and to his Church, then baptism belongs at the very heart of our worship.

There are key elements to any baptism service. The rite mirrors the initiation of Christians from the time of the early Church. The candidates are presented by being introduced as persons with names and families. If the candidates are old enough to answer for themselves, they are asked if they wish to be baptized. The people respond by welcoming these candidates, and make a commitment to uphold them in their new life in Christ. If the candidates are children, the parents and godparents speak for them and make the Decision to be baptized that the children will make again for themselves with the same words when they come to be confirmed. A prayer is said over the water, recalling God's action in human history to save us and to set us free. When all the people have expressed their common faith, the candidates are baptized with water, always in the name of the Father, and of the Son, and of the Holy

Spirit. The Commission follows, and powerful words, either for children or for adults, are used to set the newly baptized firmly within the church community. The new Christians are welcomed and the Peace is shared. The final element in the service of Holy Baptism is the Sending Out, and the people leave carrying lighted candles to express the Easter promise of resurrection that has now been given to all the baptized, as signs of the light to be carried out in mission to a dark world.

SHAPE

The Christian life is often described as the journey of faith. Baptism begins this journey with a happy moment of commitment from the candidate, from the church and from God. Grace is freely given in response to our turning to Christ. As we continue that journey, we grow and develop in our understanding of that faith and deepen our commitment in Christ. These are powerful things, and as always with God in worship, ordinary, visible signs are ways in which God acts through the liturgical ministry of the Church.

Three essential elements express the nature of any baptism service and show what God is doing. There is the sign of the cross, which is made on the forehead of the candidate. In some churches this will be made with oil, at either or both of the places where signing happens. The sign of the cross is the badge of faith, which reminds us of Christ's death for us. Just as Jesus himself was anointed with the Holy Spirit at his baptism, so the new Christian is anointed. The oil draws on its ancient use in preparing an athlete's body for a contest. The first anointing is a sign of preparation for living a Christian life. Oil has also traditionally been used in the anointing of kings, and the second anointing uses the oil of chrism (used again at confirmation) as a sign that the new Christian belongs to the community of Christ, the King of kings.

The second element – our 'drowning' in the water of baptism, where we believe we die to sin and are raised to new life – unites us to Christ's dying and rising. Water is also a sign of new life, as we are born again by water and the Spirit. This reminds us of Jesus' baptism.

The third element – the lighted candle – is a sign of the light of Christ, which has broken through the darkness of death, and is now with us as we carry his name. This candle is lit from the Paschal Candle, itself lit for the first time at Easter, and from which all baptismal candles are kindled for the year. These candles can be lit on the anniversary of baptism and serve as a reminder of both the day of baptism and the ongoing journey of faith, day by day.

SPIRIT

The Church has rediscovered the importance of Holy Baptism in the last hundred years. Baptism takes place once but has ongoing significance. In baptism we are called into an ever-growing awareness of life in Christ and within his body, the Church. The earliest Christians called their faith the Way. This teaches us that, in baptism, we are one in Christ Jesus, heirs of his spirit and fellow pilgrims on the road to glory. *Common Worship* uses this biblical framework to express this understanding. Baptism involves:

- *separation* from the world – that is, the world alienated from God;
- *reception* into a universal community centred on God, within which
- his children can *grow* into the fullness of the pattern of Christ; and
- a community whose *mission* is to serve God's Spirit in redeeming the world.

Baptism can happen in the Eucharist, in a service of the Word, or in a stand-alone service.

HOLY BAPTISM WITHIN A CELEBRATION OF HOLY COMMUNION

The Greeting

The president says:

The grace of our Lord Jesus Christ,
the love of God
and the fellowship of the Holy Spirit
be with you all

All **and also with you.**

Words of welcome or introduction may be said.

Introduction

The president may use these or other words:

Our Lord Jesus Christ has told us
that to enter the kingdom of heaven
we must be born again of water and the Spirit,
and has given us baptism as the sign and seal of this new birth.
Here we are washed by the Holy Spirit and made clean.
Here we are clothed with Christ,
dying to sin that we may live his risen life.
As children of God, we have a new dignity
and God calls us to fullness of life.

The Gloria in excelsis may be used.

The Collect

*The president introduces a period of silent prayer with the words
'Let us pray' or a more specific bidding.*

Either the Collect of the Day, or this Collect is said:

Heavenly Father,
by the power of your Holy Spirit
you give to your faithful people new life in the water of baptism.
Guide and strengthen us by the same Spirit,
that we who are born again may serve you in faith and love,
and grow into the full stature of your Son, Jesus Christ,
who is alive and reigns with you in the unity of the Holy Spirit
now and for ever.
Amen.

The Liturgy of the Word

Readings

*Either one or two readings from Scripture may precede the Gospel
reading.*

At the end of each the reader may say:

This is the word of the Lord.
All   **Thanks be to God.**

The psalm or canticle follows the first reading; other hymns and songs may be used between the readings.

Gospel Reading

An acclamation may herald the Gospel reading.

When the Gospel is announced the reader says:

Hear the Gospel of our Lord Jesus Christ according to *N*.
All **Glory to you, O Lord.**

At the end:

This is the Gospel of the Lord.
All **Praise to you, O Christ.**

Sermon

The Liturgy of Baptism

Presentation of the Candidates

The candidates may be presented to the congregation. Where appropriate, they may be presented by their godparents or sponsors.

The president asks those candidates for baptism who are able to answer for themselves:

Do you wish to be baptized?
I do.

Testimony by the candidate(s) may follow.

The president addresses the whole congregation:

Faith is the gift of God to his people.
In baptism the Lord is adding to our number
    those whom he is calling.
People of God, will you welcome these *children/candidates*
    and uphold *them* in *their* new life in Christ?
With the help of God, we will.

*At the baptism of children, the president then says to the parents
and godparents:*

Parents and godparents, the Church receives *these children*
    with joy.
Today we are trusting God for *their* growth in faith.
Will you pray for *them*,
draw *them* by your example into the community of faith
and walk with *them* in the way of Christ?
With the help of God, we will.

In baptism *these children* begin their journey in faith.
You speak for *them* today.
Will you care for *them*,
and help *them* to take *their* place
within the life and worship of Christ's Church?
With the help of God, we will.

The Decision

*A large candle may be lit. The president addresses the candidates
directly, or through their parents, godparents and sponsors:*

In baptism, God calls us out of darkness into his marvellous light.
To follow Christ means dying to sin and rising to new life with him.
Therefore I ask:

Do you reject the devil and all rebellion against God?
I reject them.

Do you renounce the deceit and corruption of evil?
I renounce them.

Do you repent of the sins that separate us from God and neighbour?
I repent of them.

Do you turn to Christ as Saviour?
I turn to Christ.

Do you submit to Christ as Lord?
I submit to Christ.

Do you come to Christ, the way, the truth and the life?
I come to Christ.

Signing with the Cross

*The president or another minister makes the sign of the cross on the
forehead of each candidate, saying:*

Christ claims you for his own.
Receive the sign of his cross.

The president may invite parents, godparents and sponsors to sign the candidates with the cross. When all the candidates have been signed, the president says:

Do not be ashamed to confess the faith of Christ crucified.
All **Fight valiantly as a disciple of Christ**
against sin, the world and the devil,
and remain faithful to Christ to the end of your life.

May almighty God deliver you from the powers of darkness,
restore in you the image of his glory,
and lead you in the light and obedience of Christ.
All **Amen.**

Prayer over the Water

The ministers and candidates gather at the baptismal font.
A canticle, psalm, hymn or litany may be used.

The president stands before the water of baptism and says:

Praise God who made heaven and earth,
All **who keeps his promise for ever.**

Let us give thanks to the Lord our God.
All **It is right to give thanks and praise.**

We thank you, almighty God, for the gift of water
to sustain, refresh and cleanse all life.
Over water the Holy Spirit moved in the beginning of creation.
Through water you led the children of Israel
from slavery in Egypt to freedom in the Promised Land.

In water your Son Jesus received the baptism of John
and was anointed by the Holy Spirit as the Messiah, the Christ,
to lead us from the death of sin to newness of life.

We thank you, Father, for the water of baptism.
In it we are buried with Christ in his death.
By it we share in his resurrection.
Through it we are reborn by the Holy Spirit.
Therefore, in joyful obedience to your Son,
we baptize into his fellowship those who come to him in faith.

Now sanctify this water that, by the power of your Holy Spirit,
they may be cleansed from sin and born again.
Renewed in your image, may they walk by the light of faith
and continue for ever in the risen life of Jesus Christ our Lord;
to whom with you and the Holy Spirit
be all honour and glory, now and for ever.

All   **Amen.**

Profession of Faith

The president addresses the congregation:

Brothers and sisters, I ask you to profess
together with *these candidates*
the faith of the Church.

Do you believe and trust in God the Father?
All   **I believe in God, the Father almighty,
creator of heaven and earth.**

Do you believe and trust in his Son Jesus Christ?

All I believe in Jesus Christ, his only Son, our Lord,
who was conceived by the Holy Spirit,
born of the Virgin Mary,
suffered under Pontius Pilate,
was crucified, died, and was buried;
he descended to the dead.
On the third day he rose again;
he ascended into heaven,
he is seated at the right hand of the Father,
and he will come to judge the living and the dead.

Do you believe and trust in the Holy Spirit?

All I believe in the Holy Spirit,
the holy catholic Church,
the communion of saints,
the forgiveness of sins,
the resurrection of the body,
and the life everlasting.
Amen.

Baptism

*If the candidate(s) can answer for themselves, the president may
say to each one:*

N, is this your faith?

Each candidate answers in their own words, or:
This is my faith.

*The president or another minister dips each candidate in water,
or pours water on them, saying:*

N, I baptize you
in the name of the Father,
and of the Son,
and of the Holy Spirit.

All **Amen.**

*If the newly baptized are clothed with a white robe, a hymn or song
may be used, and then a minister may say:*

You have been clothed with Christ.
As many as are baptized into Christ have put on Christ.

*If those who have been baptized were not signed with the cross
immediately after the Decision, the president signs each one now.*

The president says:

May God, who has received you by baptism into his Church,
pour upon you the riches of his grace,
that within the company of Christ's pilgrim people
you may daily be renewed by his anointing Spirit,
and come to the inheritance of the saints in glory.

All **Amen.**

*The president and those who have been baptized may return from
the font.*

Commission

Either:

*Where the newly baptized are unable to answer for themselves,
a minister addresses the congregation, parents and godparents,
using these or similar words:*

We have brought *these children* to baptism knowing that Jesus died and rose again for *them* and trusting in the promise that God hears and answers prayer. We have prayed that in Jesus Christ *they* will know the forgiveness of *their* sins and the new life of the Spirit.

As *they* grow up, *they* will need the help and encouragement of the Christian community, so that *they* may learn to know God in public worship and private prayer, follow Jesus Christ in the life of faith, serve *their* neighbour after the example of Christ, and in due course come to confirmation.

As part of the Church of Christ, we all have a duty to support *them* by prayer, example and teaching. As *their* parents and godparents, you have the prime responsibility for guiding and helping *them* in *their* early years. This is a demanding task for which you will need the help and grace of God. Therefore let us now pray for grace in guiding *these children* in the way of faith.

One or more of the following prayers may be used:

Faithful and loving God,
bless those who care for *these children*
and grant *them* your gifts of love, wisdom and faith.
Pour upon *them* your healing and reconciling love,
and protect *their* home from all evil.
Fill *them* with the light of your presence
and establish *them* in the joy of your kingdom,
through Jesus Christ our Lord.

All   **Amen.**

God of grace and life,
in your love you have given us
a place among your people;
keep us faithful to our baptism,

and prepare us for that glorious day
when the whole creation will be made perfect
in your Son our Saviour Jesus Christ.

All **Amen.**

These words may be added:

N and N,
today God has touched you with his love
and given you a place among his people.
God promises to be with you
in joy and in sorrow,
to be your guide in life,
and to bring you safely to heaven.
In baptism God invites you on a life-long journey.
Together with all God's people
you must explore the way of Jesus
and grow in friendship with God,
in love for his people,
and in serving others.
With us you will listen to the word of God
and receive the gifts of God.

or

*To the newly baptized who are able to answer for themselves, a
minister may say:*

Those who are baptized are called to worship and serve God.

Will you continue in the apostles' teaching and fellowship,
in the breaking of bread, and in the prayers?
With the help of God, I will.

Will you persevere in resisting evil,
and, whenever you fall into sin, repent and return to the Lord?
With the help of God, I will.

Will you proclaim by word and example
the good news of God in Christ?
With the help of God, I will.

Will you seek and serve Christ in all people,
loving your neighbour as yourself?
With the help of God, I will.

Will you acknowledge Christ's authority over human society,
by prayer for the world and its leaders,
by defending the weak, and by seeking peace and justice?
With the help of God, I will.

May Christ dwell in your heart(s) through faith,
that you may be rooted and grounded in love
and bring forth the fruit of the Spirit.
Amen.

Prayers of Intercession

*Either here or after the Welcome and Peace, intercessions may be led by
the president or others. These or other suitable words may be used. The
intercession may conclude with a Collect.*

As a royal priesthood, let us pray to the Father
through Christ who ever lives to intercede for us.

Reveal your kingdom among the nations;
may peace abound and justice flourish.
Especially for . . .

Your name be hallowed.

All **Your kingdom come.**

Send down upon us the gift of the Spirit
and renew your Church with power from on high.
Especially for . . .
Your name be hallowed.

All **Your kingdom come.**

Deliver the oppressed, strengthen the weak,
heal and restore your creation.
Especially for . . .
Your name be hallowed.

All **Your kingdom come.**

Rejoicing in the fellowship of the Church on earth,
we join our prayers with all the saints in glory.
Your name be hallowed.

All **Your kingdom come.**

The Welcome and Peace

There is one Lord, one faith, one baptism:
N and *N*, by one Spirit we are all baptized into one body.

All **We welcome you into the fellowship of faith;
we are children of the same heavenly Father;
we welcome you.**

The congregation may greet the newly baptized.

The president introduces the Peace in these or other suitable words:

We are all one in Christ Jesus.
We belong to him through faith,
heirs of the promise of the Spirit of peace.
The peace of the Lord be always with you
All **and also with you.**

A minister may say:
Let us offer one another a sign of peace.

All may exchange a sign of peace.

The Liturgy of the Eucharist

The Order for Celebration of Holy Communion continues with:

Preparation of the Table

Taking of the Bread and Wine

The Eucharistic Prayer

This short Proper Preface may be used:

And now we give you thanks
because by water and the Holy Spirit
you have made us a holy people in Jesus Christ our Lord;
you raise us to new life in him
and renew in us the image of your glory.

The Lord's Prayer

Breaking of the Bread

Giving of Communion

Prayer after Communion

The authorized Post Communion of the Day, or a seasonal form, or the following is used:

Eternal God, our beginning and our end,
preserve in your people the new life of baptism;
as Christ receives us on earth,
so may he guide us through the trials of this world
and enfold us in the joy of heaven,
where you live and reign,
one God for ever and ever.

All **Amen.**

The Sending Out

The Blessing

The president may use a seasonal blessing, or another suitable blessing, or:

The God of all grace,
who called you to his eternal glory in Christ Jesus,
establish, strengthen and settle you in the faith;
and the blessing of God almighty,
the Father, the Son, and the Holy Spirit,
be upon you and remain with you always.

All **Amen.**

Giving of a Lighted Candle

The president or another person may give each of the newly baptized a lighted candle. These may be lit from the candle used at the Decision.

When all the newly baptized have received a candle, the president says:

God has delivered us from the dominion of darkness
and has given us a place with the saints in light.

You have received the light of Christ;
walk in this light all the days of your life.

All **Shine as a light in the world
to the glory of God the Father.**

The Dismissal

Go in the light and peace of Christ.

All **Thanks be to God.**

From Easter Day to Pentecost Alleluia, alleluia *may be added to both the versicle and the response.*

CONFIRMATION OUTSIDE THE ORDER FOR CELEBRATION OF HOLY COMMUNION

This is the only liturgy contained in this book that requires the specific ministry of a bishop. The bishop is a focus of unity and the chief pastor of the worshipping community. Your bishop is most likely to visit your parish for a confirmation. More often than not, and most appropriately, a confirmation will take place within the context of the Eucharist. The text provided here is for confirmation outside the order for celebration of Holy Communion, in order to give clarity to the central aspects of the liturgy. Local tradition and the nature of a confirmation service will determine the exact content of such a service. For example, a school confirmation may be very different in nature from a main celebration on a Sunday morning in a parish. Confirmation is the mature moment of initiation and complements what takes place in baptism. Just as Jesus was baptized, so the Spirit of God rested upon him as he committed himself to his public ministry. Confirmation is the moment when adults and young people make their public affirmation of their faith and receive the empowering of the Spirit to continue their Christian journey of faith.

STRUCTURE

The candidates for confirmation will have been carefully prepared for this moment by their clergy supported by the wider community of faith. They will have been baptized or will be baptized during the course of this liturgy. They will affirm for themselves their desire to be confirmed and their belief in the faith of Jesus Christ. Candidates say again, this time for themselves, the Decision to be baptized that may have been said by parents and godparents when they were small children. The bishop leads the rite of initiation, often in his cathedral, and lays hands upon each candidate, invoking the gift of the Holy Spirit. The oil of chrism is used to 'seal' God's work in the candidates. They will often receive communion for the first time in the Confirmation Service or as soon as possible upon their return to their parish.

SHAPE

Although this service should best be in the context of the Eucharist, at St Albans Cathedral, by long tradition, it works powerfully in another setting. On Holy Saturday, the congregation gather in the darkness of the evening to hear the retelling of the salvation history – the creation, the exodus, the flood. The cathedral is full and dark and foreboding. Then, as candidates file outside into the cold night air, a new fire is lit. The Paschal Candle is prepared and brought into the nave, into the tomb, to symbolize the stirrings of the resurrection behind the closed stone of the burial place of Christ. The Exsultet is sung, everyone carries a candle, candidates are baptized and Christians are confirmed in their faith. Finally, as communion is celebrated in the morning, everyone processes through to the High Altar and, to celebrate the resurrection, a joyful sound is made. The bells ring, the organ sounds, hooters are hooted, drums are bashed, party-poppers are popped and general merrymaking and chaos is allowed, with all in their finery standing around the altar as the congregation rejoices in the resurrection of Jesus now made real and made personal in those confirmed. It is a unique occasion, culminating in the most noisy rendition of 'Thine be the glory' that can be mustered.

SPIRIT

The confirmation candidates come away from this liturgy feeling not only that something has happened to them, but that they have shared in something beyond their expectation; that is, the resurrection. To be confirmed is a wonderful thing, whatever your age. To be confirmed, or to attend a service in support of those being confirmed, is to know that God acts in our lives and that all we have to do is to turn to him and he can use our mixed bag of commitment, confusion, happiness and doubt to move us on in the great journey of faith. And when we all see our confirmation as important for ever and not just as a one-off event (rather as Easter is both once and for ever), then the Church takes on a new value and vitality.

All of us who are confirmed ought to see confirmation (and baptism) within the wider understanding of Christian initiation, of which there are five key elements:

1 **Church** – initiation enables the Church:
- to see itself as a baptized people;
- to welcome and learn from Scripture;
- to be active in mission and service;
- to expect the anointing of the Holy Spirit;
- to walk with those seeking faith;
- to stand with the despised and oppressed;
- to look for the unity of God's people.

2 **Welcome** – enquirers need a welcome:
- that is personal;
- that is public;
- that accepts their starting point;
- that expects the presence of God in their lives;
- that is willing to travel with them at their pace.

3 **Prayer** – initiation involves prayer:
- for enquirer and Church;
- to discern the presence of God;
- to open up the grace of God;
- to support the process of change;
- to discover the moments of decision;
- to receive and recognize the gifts of God.

4 **The Way** – discipleship means learning:
- to worship with the Church;
- to grow in prayer;
- to listen to the Scriptures;
- to serve our neighbour.

5 **Goal** – the goal of initiation is:
- relationship with God the Holy Trinity;
- life and worship with the Church;
- service and witness in the world.

CONFIRMATION OUTSIDE THE ORDER FOR CELEBRATION OF HOLY COMMUNION

Preparation

The Greeting

The bishop greets the people, using these or other suitable words:

Blessed be God, Father, Son and Holy Spirit.
All **Blessed be his kingdom, now and for ever.**
Amen.

or from Easter Day to Pentecost:

Alleluia. Christ is risen.
All **He is risen indeed. Alleluia.**

There is one body and one spirit.
All **There is one hope to which we were called;**
one Lord, one faith, one baptism,
All **one God and Father of all.**

Peace be with you.
All **And also with you.**

The bishop may introduce the service.

Gloria in excelsis may be used.

The Collect

*The bishop introduces a period of silent prayer with the words
'Let us pray' or a more specific bidding.*

*The Collect of the Day is normally used on Sundays and on
Principal Festivals. On other occasions a seasonal Collect or this
prayer is used:*

Heavenly Father,
by the power of your Holy Spirit
you give to your faithful people new life in the water of baptism.
Guide and strengthen us by the same Spirit,
that we who are born again may serve you in faith and love,
and grow into the full stature of your Son, Jesus Christ,
who is alive and reigns with you in the unity of the Holy Spirit
now and for ever.

All   **Amen.**

The Liturgy of the Word

*The readings of the day are normally used on Sundays and
Principal Festivals.*

*Either one or two readings from Scripture may precede the Gospel
reading. At the end of each the reader may say:*

This is the word of the Lord.
All   **Thanks be to God.**

*The psalm or canticle follows the first reading; other hymns and
songs may be used between the readings.*

Gospel Reading

An acclamation may herald the Gospel reading.
When the Gospel is announced the reader says:

Hear the Gospel of our Lord Jesus Christ according to *N*.

All **Glory to you, O Lord.**

At the end:

This is the Gospel of the Lord.

All **Praise to you, O Christ.**

Sermon

The Liturgy of Initiation

Presentation of the Candidates

The candidates may be presented to the congregation. Where
appropriate, they may be presented by their godparents or sponsors.

The bishop asks the candidates:

Have you been baptized in the name of the Father, and of the Son,
and of the Holy Spirit?
I have.

Are you ready with your own mouth and from your own heart to
affirm your faith in Jesus Christ?
I am.

Testimony by the candidates may follow.

The bishop addresses the whole congregation:

People of God, will you welcome *these candidates* and uphold *them* in *their* life in Christ?

All   **With the help of God, we will.**

The Decision

A large candle may be lit. The bishop addresses all the candidates:

In baptism, God calls us out of darkness into his marvellous light. To follow Christ means dying to sin and rising to new life with him. Therefore I ask:

Do you reject the devil and all rebellion against God?
I reject them.

Do you renounce the deceit and corruption of evil?
I renounce them.

Do you repent of the sins that separate us from God and neighbour?
I repent of them.

Do you turn to Christ as Saviour?
I turn to Christ.

Do you submit to Christ as Lord?
I submit to Christ.

Do you come to Christ, the way, the truth and the life?
I come to Christ.

The bishop says:

May God who has given you the desire to follow Christ
give you strength to continue in the Way.
Amen.

*The ministers and candidates for confirmation gather at the
baptismal font. A canticle, psalm, hymn or a litany may be used.*

Profession of Faith

The bishop addresses the congregation:

Brothers and sisters, I ask you to profess
together with *these candidates*
the faith of the Church.

Do you believe and trust in God the Father?
All   **I believe in God, the Father almighty,
creator of heaven and earth.**

Do you believe and trust in his Son Jesus Christ?
All   **I believe in Jesus Christ, his only Son, our Lord,
who was conceived by the Holy Spirit,
born of the Virgin Mary,
suffered under Pontius Pilate,
was crucified, died, and was buried;
he descended to the dead.
On the third day he rose again;
he ascended into heaven,
he is seated at the right hand of the Father,
and he will come to judge the living and the dead.**

Do you believe and trust in the Holy Spirit?

All **I believe in the Holy Spirit,**
the holy catholic Church,
the communion of saints,
the forgiveness of sins,
the resurrection of the body,
and the life everlasting.
Amen.

The candidates may come forward to the font and sign themselves
with water, or the bishop may sprinkle them.

Then the bishop says:

Almighty God,
we thank you for our fellowship in the household of faith
with all who have been baptized into your name.
Keep us faithful to our baptism,
and so make us ready for that day
when the whole creation shall be made perfect in your Son,
our Saviour Jesus Christ.

All **Amen.**

The bishop and the candidates gather at the place of confirmation.
A hymn, chant or litany may be used.

Confirmation

The bishop stands before those who are to be confirmed, and says:

Our help is in the name of the Lord

All **who has made heaven and earth.**

Blessed be the name of the Lord

All **now and for ever. Amen.**

The bishop extends his hands towards those to be confirmed and says:

Almighty and ever-living God,
you have given these your servants new birth
in baptism by water and the Spirit,
and have forgiven them all their sins.
Let your Holy Spirit rest upon them:
the Spirit of wisdom and understanding;
the Spirit of counsel and inward strength;
the Spirit of knowledge and true godliness;
and let their delight be in the fear of the Lord.

All   Amen.

The bishop addresses each candidate by name:

N, God has called you by name and made you his own.

He then lays his hand on the head of each, saying:

Confirm, O Lord, your servant with your Holy Spirit.

All   Amen.

The bishop invites the congregation to pray for all those on whom hands have been laid:

All   Defend, O Lord, these your servants with your heavenly grace,
that they may continue yours for ever,
and daily increase in your Holy Spirit more and more
until they come to your everlasting kingdom.
Amen.

Commission

The bishop may use this Commission:

Those who are baptized are called to worship and serve God.

Will you continue in the apostles' teaching and fellowship,
in the breaking of bread, and in the prayers?
With the help of God, I will.

Will you persevere in resisting evil,
and, whenever you fall into sin, repent and return to the Lord?
With the help of God, I will.

Will you proclaim by word and example
the good news of God in Christ?
With the help of God, I will.

Will you seek and serve Christ in all people,
loving your neighbour as yourself?
With the help of God, I will.

Will you acknowledge Christ's authority over human society,
by prayer for the world and its leaders,
by defending the weak, and by seeking peace and justice?
With the help of God, I will.

May Christ dwell in your hearts through faith,
that you may be rooted and grounded in love
and bring forth the fruit of the Spirit.
All   **Amen.**

The Peace

The bishop introduces the Peace in these or other suitable words:

God has made us one in Christ.
He has set his seal upon us and, as a pledge of what is to come,
has given the Spirit to dwell in our hearts.

The peace of the Lord be always with you.
All **And also with you.**

A minister may say:

Let us offer one another a sign of peace.

All may exchange a sign of peace.

Prayers

*The service continues with suitable prayers, ending with the Lord's
Prayer. It is appropriate that the newly confirmed take their part in
leading the prayers. The prayers provided in the service of Holy
Baptism or in the service of Confirmation may be used.*

The Sending Out

The Blessing

The bishop may use a seasonal blessing, or another suitable blessing.

or

The God of all grace,
who called you to his eternal glory in Christ Jesus,
establish, strengthen and settle you in the faith;
and the blessing of God almighty,
the Father, the Son and the Holy Spirit,
be upon you and remain with you always.

All **Amen.**

The Dismissal

Go in the light and peace of Christ.

All **Thanks be to God.**

From Easter to Pentecost, Alleluia, alleluia *may be added after
both the versicle and response.*

The bishop may lead the newly confirmed through the church.

THE MARRIAGE SERVICE

When the liturgy was revised, the service that was changed the least was the Marriage Service. The rite that has joined couples for centuries still exists, in essentially the same form, in the modern liturgy of the Church. Ironically, apart from the Christmas carol services, the Marriage Service is still probably the act of worship most attended by the least regular churchgoers. This rite of passage is important for each couple and important for the life of the Church. And, as many misleading preconceptions and media images of weddings abound, it is important that all faithful Anglicans know what is in the Marriage Service and what is not. Marriage matters.

STRUCTURE

The first point here is that an obligation is laid upon a church to ensure that marriage preparation takes place for every couple married in that church. Personal choice and professional help from the priest will make every wedding unique and personal.

The wedding service starts with a welcome, after which the Preface is read. This summarizes both the theological understanding of Christian marriage and the valuable reasons why marriage exists in society. Following the Liturgy of the Word, the couple are invited to exchange solemn vows and rings. The marriage is proclaimed before the priest has done anything. The Blessing follows. The Nuptial Blessing prayer is one of the best in *Common Worship*. The registration is a formal part of the service and is preferably done in the sight of the people. Finally, husband and wife are sent out as a new creation into God's world.

SHAPE

Couples really do come in all shapes and sizes. Every wedding, like every marriage, is unique. But weddings are more than simply acts of worship or legal contracts. God, who is love, is involved, and his grace allows the couple to take centre stage for a moment. The couple become ministers of the sacrament to each other, making their marriage happen by the exchange both of vows and rings. They become priests to each other as they change from man and woman to husband and wife. This is true not just for their special day but for every day of their married life. The sacrificial nature of the marriage relationship is embodied in the liturgy and is a foretaste of the relationship we shall share with God in the Holy Trinity.

SPIRIT

In John 2 Jesus performs his first miracle at a wedding in Cana of Galilee. It is perhaps the most obvious wedding Gospel reading, and is suggested by *Common Worship*. Jesus performs his first miracle to begin to show us who he is and to affirm that God is present in our most intimate human relationships. In the changing of the water into wine, Jesus points towards the cross, and the miracle of the resurrection when death becomes life. This is the promise made to all of us, and in marriage when man and woman change and become husband and wife – in biblical terms, one flesh – God gives a unique insight into the meaning of sacrificial love.

Those planning a wedding may like to look at alternative vows on <www.cofe.anglican.org/worship/liturgy/commonworship/texts/marriage/alternativetexts.html#vows>.

THE MARRIAGE SERVICE

The Welcome

The minister welcomes the people using these or other appropriate words:

The grace of our Lord Jesus Christ,
the love of God,
and the fellowship of the Holy Spirit
be with you

All **and also with you.**

This sentence may be used:

God is love, and those who live in love live in God
and God lives in them. (1 John 4.16)

This prayer may be said:

All **God of wonder and of joy:**
grace comes from you,
and you alone are the source of life and love.
Without you, we cannot please you;
without your love, our deeds are worth nothing.
Send your Holy Spirit,
and pour into our hearts
that most excellent gift of love,
that we may worship you now

with thankful hearts
and serve you always with willing minds;
through Jesus Christ our Lord.
Amen.

A hymn may be sung.

Preface

In the presence of God, Father, Son and Holy Spirit,
we have come together
to witness the marriage of *N* and *N*,
to pray for God's blessing on them,
to share their joy
and to celebrate their love.

Marriage is a gift of God in creation
through which husband and wife may know the grace of God.
It is given
that as man and woman grow together in love and trust,
they shall be united with one another in heart, body and mind,
as Christ is united with his bride, the Church.

The gift of marriage brings husband and wife together
in the delight and tenderness of sexual union
and joyful commitment to the end of their lives.
It is given as the foundation of family life
in which children are [born and] nurtured
and in which each member of the family,
    in good times and in bad,
may find strength, companionship and comfort,
and grow to maturity in love.

Marriage is a way of life made holy by God,
and blessed by the presence of our Lord Jesus Christ
with those celebrating a wedding at Cana in Galilee.
Marriage is a sign of unity and loyalty
which all should uphold and honour.
It enriches society and strengthens community.
No one should enter into it lightly or selfishly
but reverently and responsibly in the sight of almighty God.

N and *N* are now to enter this way of life.
They will each give their consent to the other
and make solemn vows,
and in token of this they will [each] give and receive a ring.
We pray with them that the Holy Spirit will guide
    and strengthen them,
that they may fulfil God's purposes
for the whole of their earthly life together.

The Declarations

The minister says to the congregation:

First, I am required to ask anyone present who knows a reason
why these persons may not lawfully marry, to declare it now.

The minister says to the couple:

The vows you are about to take are to be made in the presence
    of God,
who is judge of all and knows all the secrets of our hearts;
therefore if either of you knows a reason why you may not
    lawfully marry,
you must declare it now.

The minister says to the bridegroom:

N, will you take N to be your wife?
Will you love her, comfort her, honour and protect her,
and, forsaking all others,
be faithful to her as long as you both shall live?

He answers:

I will.

The minister says to the bride:

N, will you take N to be your husband?
Will you love him, comfort him, honour and protect him,
and, forsaking all others,
be faithful to him as long as you both shall live?

She answers:

I will.

The minister says to the congregation:

Will you, the families and friends of N and N,
support and uphold them in their marriage
now and in the years to come?

All **We will.**

The Collect

The minister invites the people to pray, silence is kept and the minister says the Collect:

God our Father,
from the beginning
you have blessed creation with abundant life.
Pour out your blessings upon *N* and *N*,
that they may be joined in mutual love and companionship,
in holiness and commitment to each other.
We ask this through our Lord Jesus Christ your Son,
who is alive and reigns with you,
in the unity of the Holy Spirit,
one God, now and for ever.

All **Amen.**

Readings

At least one reading from the Bible is used.

Sermon

The Marriage

A hymn may be sung.

The couple stand before the minister.

The Vows

The minister introduces the vows in these or similar words:

N and N, I now invite you to join hands and make your vows,
in the presence of God and his people.

The bride and bridegroom face each other.
The bridegroom takes the bride's right hand in his.

I, N, take you, N,
to be my wife,
to have and to hold
from this day forward;
for better, for worse,
for richer, for poorer,
in sickness and in health,
to love and to cherish,
till death us do part;
according to God's holy law.
In the presence of God I make this vow.

They loose hands.
The bride takes the bridegroom's right hand in hers, and says:

I, N, take you, N,
to be my husband,
to have and to hold
from this day forward;
for better, for worse,
for richer, for poorer,
in sickness and in health,
to love and to cherish,

till death us do part;
according to God's holy law.
In the presence of God I make this vow.

They loose hands.

The Giving of Rings

The minister receives the ring(s), and says this prayer:

Heavenly Father, by your blessing
let *these rings* be to N and N
a symbol of unending love and faithfulness,
to remind them of the vow and covenant
which they have made this day
through Jesus Christ our Lord.

All **Amen.**

The bridegroom places the ring on the fourth finger of the bride's left hand and, holding it there, says:

N, I give you this ring
as a sign of our marriage.
With my body I honour you,
all that I am I give to you,
and all that I have I share with you,
within the love of God,
Father, Son and Holy Spirit.

If rings are exchanged, they loose hands and the bride places a ring on the fourth finger of the bridegroom's left hand and, holding it there, says:

N, I give you this ring
as a sign of our marriage.
With my body I honour you,
all that I am I give to you,
and all that I have I share with you,
within the love of God,
Father, Son and Holy Spirit.

If only one ring is used, before they loose hands the bride says:

N, I receive this ring
as a sign of our marriage.
With my body I honour you,
all that I am I give to you,
and all that I have I share with you,
within the love of God,
Father, Son and Holy Spirit.

The Proclamation

The minister addresses the people:

In the presence of God, and before this congregation,
N and *N* have given their consent
and made their marriage vows to each other.
They have declared their marriage by the joining of hands
and by the giving and receiving of *rings.*
I therefore proclaim that they are husband and wife.

The minister joins their right hands together and says:

Those whom God has joined together let no one put asunder.

The Blessing of the Marriage

*The husband and wife kneel. The minister may use the
following blessing:*

Blessed are you, O Lord our God,
for you have created joy and gladness,
pleasure and delight, love, peace and fellowship.
Pour out the abundance of your blessing
upon *N* and *N* in their new life together.
Let their love for each other be a seal upon their hearts
and a crown upon their heads.
Bless them in their work and in their companionship;
awake and asleep,
in joy and in sorrow,
in life and in death.
Finally, in your mercy, bring them to that banquet
where your saints feast for ever in your heavenly home.
We ask this through Jesus Christ your Son, our Lord,
who lives and reigns with you and the Holy Spirit,
one God, now and for ever.

All   **Amen.**

The minister says to the couple:

God the Father,
God the Son,
God the Holy Spirit,
bless, preserve and keep you;
the Lord mercifully grant you the riches of his grace,
that you may please him both in body and soul,
and, living together in faith and love,
may receive the blessings of eternal life.

All   **Amen.**

Registration of the Marriage

A hymn or psalm may be used.

Prayers

These or other suitable prayers are used. The prayers usually include these concerns and may follow this sequence:

Thanksgiving

Spiritual growth

Faithfulness, joy, love, forgiveness and healing

Children, other family members and friends

Faithful God,
holy and eternal,
source of life and spring of love,
we thank and praise you for bringing *N* and *N* to this day,
and we pray for them.
Lord of life and love:

All **hear our prayer.**

May their marriage be life-giving and life-long,
enriched by your presence and strengthened by your grace;
may they bring comfort and confidence to each other
in faithfulness and trust.
Lord of life and love:

All **hear our prayer.**

May the hospitality of their home
bring refreshment and joy to all around them;
may their love overflow to neighbours in need
and embrace those in distress.

Lord of life and love:

All **hear our prayer.**

May they discern in your word
order and purpose for their lives;
and may the power of your Holy Spirit
lead them in truth and defend them in adversity.
Lord of life and love:

All **hear our prayer.**

May they nurture their family with devotion,
see their children grow in body, mind and spirit
and come at last to the end of their lives
with hearts content and in joyful anticipation of heaven.
Lord of life and love:

All **hear our prayer.**

The prayers conclude with the Lord's Prayer.

As our Saviour taught us, so we pray

All **Our Father in heaven,**
hallowed be your name,
your kingdom come,
your will be done,
on earth as in heaven.
Give us today our daily bread.
Forgive us our sins
as we forgive those who sin against us.
Lead us not into temptation
but deliver us from evil.
For the kingdom, the power,
and the glory are yours
now and for ever.
Amen.

or

Let us pray with confidence as our Saviour has taught us

All Our Father, who art in heaven,
hallowed be thy name;
thy kingdom come;
thy will be done;
on earth as it is in heaven.
Give us this day our daily bread.
And forgive us our trespasses,
as we forgive those who trespass against us.
And lead us not into temptation;
but deliver us from evil.
For thine is the kingdom,
the power and the glory,
for ever and ever.
Amen.

A hymn may be sung.

The Dismissal

The minister says:

God the Holy Trinity make *you* strong in faith and love,
defend *you* on every side, and guide *you* in truth and peace;
and the blessing of God almighty,
the Father, the Son, and the Holy Spirit,
be among *you* and remain with *you* always.

All Amen.

THE FUNERAL SERVICE

We all tend to remember the funerals we have attended. If a funeral, the final liturgy of the deceased, is done well, mourners can come away with the somewhat incongruous remark that they 'enjoyed that service'. Enjoyment is not usually a funeral response, but what is meant here is that the funeral did its job for them and for the person they knew and loved. Laughter and tears are very close emotions, and they sum up the reality of life and death. A funeral is a liturgy that, more than any other, meets people where they are and seeks to point them to the Christian hope in the resurrection.

STRUCTURE

Common Worship seeks to widen the funeral experience from a short one-off liturgy into a more realistic acknowledgement of what really takes place around death. Liturgy is provided for a variety of pastoral moments, and the wise minister will adapt it to the specific circumstances. Texts are provided for Ministry at the Time of Death, Before the Funeral, the Funeral itself and After the Funeral, reflecting and resourcing the situations we all find ourselves in at these sad times. The Funeral Service itself has a great deal of in-built flexibility to enable individual and corporate expression to be valued. Symbols of a person's faith or life may be placed on or around the coffin, and tributes may be given. There is an opportunity for reflection and repentance. The key elements of a funeral are the Commendation – the giving back to God of the deceased person – and the Committal – the act of finally letting go of the body or ashes. Both are represented by formal words. A proper service is also available for the Funeral of a Child, and, for the first time, a Memorial Service is provided.

SHAPE

There are many types of funeral; every funeral is unique and equally important. I have taken the whole range of funerals, from the pauper's funeral when the funeral director and I were the only people present, to the full-blown military funeral with thousands present. Each funeral demands the same care and attention. Each funeral though has, to a greater or lesser extent, a pattern for those who are in need of the Church's ministry. First and foremost, a funeral is for the deceased person, who must be treated with respect and honesty. The funeral is for family and friends to have the opportunity to say farewell with gladness and thanksgiving in their hearts. This cannot always be so, and sometimes it is very important to acknowledge anguish, but it is worth noting that *Common Worship* tries hard to make the needs of the bereaved central. The people who are left are important to God; he can deal with the one who is at rest in his own way and through the promises of Jesus. A funeral is also a community event. Sometimes it will be an event for the church family as well, but most often there is an aspect of every funeral that recognizes the deceased person's place in society.

There is a simple fact about the *Common Worship* service that signifies the way in which the liturgy tries to honour the person who has died and stand alongside the bereaved. In the Book of Common Prayer the deceased is never referred to by name, only as brother or sister. The *Common Worship* liturgy, by contrast, names the deceased to indicate that the Funeral Service is about a real person and real friends and family who now stand before God on earth and in heaven at one of the most important times ever for them all.

SPIRIT

The Funeral Service looks backward in grief and forward in hope. The liturgy is about resurrection. This is the Christian hope, and the liturgy commends all our doubts and fears to God so that he can do what only he does for us. *Common Worship* is not about judgement and damnation; these are real enough but are best considered on their own. The service is about continuing the journey of faith, either for the dead person, who we now hope stands in glory, or for those of us who are left, who can recommit themselves to live God's way here on earth. At a funeral, we often have nothing left or find that words are just not enough. This liturgy seeks to give us the framework and the words to help us to rely upon God's compassion and his ultimate gift. This is, after all, a true faith and a sure hope.

THE FUNERAL SERVICE

Pastoral Introduction

This may be read by those present before the service begins.

God's love and power extend over all creation. Every life, including our own, is precious to God. Christians have always believed that there is hope in death as in life, and that there is new life in Christ over death.

Even those who share such faith find that there is a real sense of loss at the death of a loved one. We will each have had our own experiences of their life and death, with different memories and different feelings of love, grief and respect. To acknowledge this at the beginning of the service should help us to use this occasion to express our faith and our feelings as we say farewell, to acknowledge our loss and our sorrow, and to reflect on our own mortality. Those who mourn need support and consolation. Our presence here today is part of that continuing support.

The Gathering

The coffin may be received by the minister. One or more sentences of Scripture may be used:

'I am the resurrection and the life,' says the Lord. 'Those who believe in me, even though they die, will live, and everyone who lives and believes in me will never die.' (John 11.25, 26)

I am convinced that neither death, nor life, nor angels, nor rulers, nor things present, nor things to come, nor powers, nor height, nor depth, nor anything else in all creation, will be able to separate us from the love of God in Christ Jesus our Lord. (Romans 8.38, 39)

Since we believe that Jesus died and rose again, even so, through Jesus, God will bring with him those who have died. So we will be with the Lord for ever. Therefore encourage one another with these words. (1 Thessalonians 4.14, 17b, 18)

We brought nothing into the world, and we take nothing out. The Lord gave, and the Lord has taken away; blessed be the name of the Lord. (1 Timothy 6.7; Job 1.21b)

The steadfast love of the Lord never ceases, his mercies never come to an end; they are new every morning; great is his faithfulness. (Lamentations 3.22, 23)

Blessed are those who mourn, for they will be comforted. (Matthew 5.4)

God so loved the world that he gave his only Son, so that everyone who believes in him may not perish but may have eternal life. (John 3.16)

Introduction

The minister says:

We meet in the name of Jesus Christ,
who died and was raised to the glory of God the Father.
Grace and mercy be with you.

The minister introduces the service in these or other suitable words:

We have come here today
to remember before God our *brother/sister N*;
to give thanks for *his/her* life;
to commend *him/her* to God our merciful redeemer and judge;
to commit *his/her* body to be *buried/cremated*,
and to comfort one another in our grief.

The minister may say one of these prayers:

God of all consolation,
your Son Jesus Christ was moved to tears
at the grave of Lazarus his friend.
Look with compassion on your children in their loss;
give to troubled hearts the light of hope
and strengthen in us the gift of faith,
in Jesus Christ our Lord.

All **Amen.**

or

Almighty God,
you judge us with infinite mercy and justice
and love everything you have made.
In your mercy
turn the darkness of death into the dawn of new life,

and the sorrow of parting into the joy of heaven;
through our Saviour, Jesus Christ.

All **Amen.**

A hymn may be sung.
A brief tribute may be made.

Prayers of Penitence

These or similar words may be used to introduce the confession:

As children of a loving heavenly Father,
let us ask his forgiveness,
for he is gentle and full of compassion.

Silence may be kept.

These words may be used:

God of mercy,
we acknowledge that we are all sinners.
We turn from the wrong that we have thought and said and done,
and are mindful of all that we have failed to do.
For the sake of Jesus, who died for us,
forgive us for all that is past,
and help us to live each day
in the light of Christ our Lord.

All **Amen.**

or

Lord, have mercy.

All **Lord, have mercy.**

Christ, have mercy.

All **Christ, have mercy.**

Lord, have mercy.

All **Lord, have mercy.**

The minister may say:

May God our Father forgive us our sins
and bring us to the eternal joy of his kingdom,
where dust and ashes have no dominion.

All **Amen.**

The Collect

*The minister invites the people to pray, silence is kept and the
minister says this or another suitable Collect:*

Merciful Father,
hear our prayers and comfort us;
renew our trust in your Son,
whom you raised from the dead;
strengthen our faith
that all who have died in the love of Christ
will share in his resurrection;
who lives and reigns with you,
in the unity of the Holy Spirit,
one God, now and for ever.

All **Amen.**

A reading from the Old or New Testament may be read.

This or another psalm or hymn is used:

1 The Lord is my shepherd; ◆
  therefore can I lack nothing.

2 He makes me lie down in green pastures ◆
  and leads me beside still waters.

3 He shall refresh my soul ◆
  and guide me in the paths of righteousness for his name's sake.

4 Though I walk through the valley of the shadow of death,
    I will fear no evil; ◆
  for you are with me; your rod and your staff, they comfort me.

5 You spread a table before me
    in the presence of those who trouble me; ◆
  you have anointed my head with oil and my cup shall be full.

6 Surely goodness and loving mercy shall follow me
    all the days of my life, ◆
  and I will dwell in the house of the Lord for ever. (Psalm 23)

*A reading from the New Testament (which may be a Gospel reading)
is used.*

A sermon is preached.

Prayers

A minister leads the prayers of the people.
The prayers usually follow this sequence:

> *Thanksgiving for the life of the departed*
>
> *Prayer for those who mourn*
>
> *Prayers of Penitence (if not already used)*
>
> *Prayer for readiness to live in the light of eternity*

This form may be used:

God of mercy, Lord of life,
you have made us in your image
to reflect your truth and light:
we give you thanks for *N*,
for the grace and mercy *he/she* received from you,
for all that was good in *his/her* life,
for the memories we treasure today.
Especially we thank you . . .

Silence

Lord, in your mercy
All **hear our prayer.**

You promised eternal life to those who believe.
Remember for good this your servant *N*
as we also remember *him/her*.
Bring all who rest in Christ
into the fullness of your kingdom
where sins have been forgiven
and death is no more.

Silence

Lord, in your mercy
All   **hear our prayer.**

Your mighty power brings joy out of grief
and life out of death.
Look in mercy on . . . *and* all who mourn.
Give them patient faith in times of darkness.
Strengthen them with the knowledge of your love.

Silence

Lord, in your mercy
All   **hear our prayer.**

You are tender towards your children
and your mercy is over all your works.
Heal the memories of hurt and failure.
Give us the wisdom and grace to use aright
the time that is left to us here on earth,
to turn to Christ and follow in his steps
in the way that leads to everlasting life.

Silence

Lord, in your mercy
All   **hear our prayer.**

All   **God of mercy,**
entrusting into your hands all that you have made
and rejoicing in our communion with all your faithful people,
we make our prayers through Jesus Christ our Saviour. Amen.

The Lord's Prayer may be said.
As our Saviour taught us, so we pray

All   Our Father in heaven,
     hallowed be your name,
     your kingdom come,
     your will be done,
     on earth as in heaven.
     Give us today our daily bread.
     Forgive us our sins
     as we forgive those who sin against us.
     Lead us not into temptation
     but deliver us from evil.
     For the kingdom, the power,
     and the glory are yours
     now and for ever.
     Amen.

   or

   Let us pray with confidence as our Saviour has taught us

All   Our Father, who art in heaven,
     hallowed be thy name;
     thy kingdom come;
     thy will be done;
     on earth as it is in heaven.
     Give us this day our daily bread.
     And forgive us our trespasses,
     as we forgive those who trespass against us.
     And lead us not into temptation;
     but deliver us from evil.
     For thine is the kingdom,
     the power and the glory,
     for ever and ever.
     Amen.

   A hymn may be sung.

Commendation and Farewell

The minister stands by the coffin and may invite others to gather around it.

The minister says:

Let us commend *N* to the mercy of God,
our maker and redeemer.

Silence is kept.

The minister uses this or another prayer of entrusting and commending.

God our creator and redeemer,
by your power Christ conquered death
and entered into glory.
Confident of his victory
and claiming his promises,
we entrust *N* to your mercy
in the name of Jesus our Lord,
who died and is alive
and reigns with you,
now and for ever.

All **Amen.**

The Committal

Sentences of Scripture may be used.

The minister says:

either

The Lord is full of compassion and mercy,
slow to anger and of great goodness.
As a father is tender towards his children,
so is the Lord tender to those that fear him.
For he knows of what we are made;
he remembers that we are but dust.
Our days are like the grass;
we flourish like a flower of the field;
when the wind goes over it, it is gone
and its place will know it no more.
But the merciful goodness of the Lord endures for ever and ever
   toward those that fear him
and his righteousness upon their children's children.

or

We have but a short time to live.
Like a flower we blossom and then wither;
like a shadow we flee and never stay.
In the midst of life we are in death;
to whom can we turn for help,
but to you, Lord, who are justly angered by our sins?
Yet, Lord God most holy, Lord most mighty,
O holy and most merciful Saviour,
deliver us from the bitter pain of eternal death.
Lord, you know the secrets of our hearts;
hear our prayer, O God most mighty;
spare us, most worthy judge eternal;
at our last hour let us not fall from you,
O holy and merciful Saviour.

The minister uses one of the following forms of Committal.

At the burial of a body:

We have entrusted our *brother/sister N* to God's mercy,
and we now commit *his/her* body to the ground:
earth to earth, ashes to ashes, dust to dust:
in sure and certain hope of the resurrection to eternal life
through our Lord Jesus Christ,
who will transform our frail bodies
that they may be conformed to his glorious body,
who died, was buried, and rose again for us.
To him be glory for ever.

All   **Amen.**

or

In a crematorium, if the Committal is to follow at the Burial of the Ashes:

We have entrusted our *brother/sister N* to God's mercy,
and now, in preparation for burial,
we give *his/her* body to be cremated.
We look for the fullness of the resurrection
when Christ shall gather all his saints
to reign with him in glory for ever.

All   **Amen.**

or

In a crematorium, if the Committal is to take place then:

We have entrusted our *brother/sister N* to God's mercy,
and we now commit *his/her* body to be cremated:
earth to earth, ashes to ashes, dust to dust:
in sure and certain hope of the resurrection to eternal life
through our Lord Jesus Christ,

who will transform our frail bodies
that they may be conformed to his glorious body,
who died, was buried, and rose again for us.
To him be glory for ever.

All   **Amen.**

The Dismissal

This may include:

> *The Lord's Prayer (if not used earlier)*
> *The Nunc dimittis*
> *One or more suitable prayers*
> *An Ending*

The Lord's Prayer

As our Saviour taught us, so we pray

All   **Our Father in heaven,**
hallowed be your name,
your kingdom come,
your will be done,
on earth as in heaven.
Give us today our daily bread.
Forgive us our sins
as we forgive those who sin against us.
Lead us not into temptation
but deliver us from evil.
For the kingdom, the power,
and the glory are yours
now and for ever.
Amen.

or

Let us pray with confidence as our Saviour has taught us

All   Our Father, who art in heaven,
hallowed be thy name;
thy kingdom come;
thy will be done;
on earth as it is in heaven.
Give us this day our daily bread.
And forgive us our trespasses,
as we forgive those who trespass against us.
And lead us not into temptation;
but deliver us from evil.
For thine is the kingdom,
the power and the glory,
for ever and ever.
Amen.

Nunc dimittis (The Song of Simeon)

(A diamond at the end of a line indicates a brief pause.)

1   Now, Lord, you let your servant go in peace: ◆
your word has been fulfilled.

2   My own eyes have seen the salvation ◆
which you have prepared in the sight of every people;

3   A light to reveal you to the nations ◆
and the glory of your people Israel. (Luke 2.29–32)

Glory to the Father and to the Son
and to the Holy Spirit;
as it was in the beginning is now
and shall be for ever. Amen.

One or more of these prayers, or other suitable prayers, may be used:

All Heavenly Father,
in your Son Jesus Christ
you have given us a true faith and a sure hope.
Strengthen this faith and hope in us all our days,
that we may live as those who believe in
the communion of saints,
the forgiveness of sins
and the resurrection to eternal life;
through Jesus Christ our Lord.
Amen.

All God be in my head,
and in my understanding;
God be in my eyes,
and in my looking;
God be in my mouth,
and in my speaking;
God be in my heart,
and in my thinking;
God be at my end,
and at my departing.
Amen.

Support us, O Lord,
all the day long of this troublous life,
until the shadows lengthen and the evening comes,
the busy world is hushed,
the fever of life is over
and our work is done.
Then, Lord, in your mercy grant us a safe lodging,

a holy rest, and peace at the last;
through Christ our Lord.

All **Amen.**

Ending

One of these, or another suitable ending, may be used:

May God in his infinite love and mercy
bring the whole Church,
living and departed in the Lord Jesus,
to a joyful resurrection
and the fulfilment of his eternal kingdom.

All **Amen.**

May God give *you*
his comfort and his peace,
his light and his joy,
in this world and the next;
and the blessing of God almighty,
the Father, the Son, and the Holy Spirit,
be among you and remain with you always.

All **Amen.**

God will show us the path of life;
in his presence is the fullness of joy:
and at his right hand
there is pleasure for evermore. (cf. Psalm 16.11)

Unto him that is able to keep us from falling,
and to present us faultless before the presence of his glory
    with exceeding joy,
to the only wise God our Saviour,
be glory and majesty,
dominion and power,
both now and ever. (Jude 24, 25)

All **Amen.**

AN ORDER FOR NIGHT PRAYER (COMPLINE)

Things always seem worse at night. It's something about the darkness, the slow passing of the hours and the fear of the unknown. And yet night-time can be beautiful, can be celebratory and can be awe-inspiring. Our feelings about the night go all the way back to creation and God breaking into chaos to bring order and life. We regularly speak about God as light and of how his love for us brings light into our lives. So the darkness needs consecrating to his glory. The ordering of time has been a Christian practice since the earliest days of the Church.

Daily Morning and Evening Prayer are still an obligation placed upon the clergy. Praying regularly is an obligation placed upon every Christian. Compline, or Night Prayer, is a beneficial way in which to complete a day.

STRUCTURE

Common Worship gives an order for Night Prayer that can be used at the very end of the day, either in a service or when alone. It has a wonderful resonance that feels somehow calming and safe. Using ancient words, the liturgy provides an opportunity to confess the wrong-doings of the day, to commend ourselves into the care of

God and to use those powerful words of Simeon, the Nunc dimittis. This short time of prayer concludes with a prayer of protection and an anticipation of the dawn – another day that will be God's.

SHAPE

So much of our worship is about what we can do or say in relation to God. Night Prayer is about what he does for us. We hand ourselves over to sleep, the mini-death, and we hope for the new day. This 'office' is all about our total reliance upon God and our confidence in his strength.

SPIRIT

God has always broken into darkness. In creation, God brings light. When the angels sang at night, and the star shone above Bethlehem, the shepherds and the Magi were guided to see the Word made flesh, born into the darkness to be the Light of the World. After the tomb had been sealed up, the stirrings of life began, and when Mary Magdalene came to the tomb at dawn, the stone had been rolled away and Jesus was not there. The creation, the incarnation and the resurrection all took place at night. God acts when we are at our weakest and most helpless. Ending the evening in prayer is the right way to end the day and the right way to rely upon God who is Father, Son and Holy Spirit. 'The Lord almighty grant us a quiet night and a perfect end.'

AN ORDER FOR NIGHT PRAYER (COMPLINE)

Preparation

The Lord almighty grant us a quiet night and a perfect end.

All **Amen.**

Our help is in the name of the Lord

All **who made heaven and earth.**

A period of silence for reflection on the past day may follow.

The following or other suitable words of penitence may be used:

All **Most merciful God,**
we confess to you,
before the whole company of heaven and one another,
that we have sinned in thought, word and deed
and in what we have failed to do.
Forgive us our sins,
heal us by your Spirit
and raise us to new life in Christ.
Amen.

O God, make speed to save us.

All **O Lord, make haste to help us.**

All   Glory to the Father and to the Son
        and to the Holy Spirit;
        as it was in the beginning is now
        and shall be for ever. Amen.
        Alleluia.

The following or another suitable hymn may be sung:

All   Before the ending of the day,
        Creator of the world, we pray
        That you, with steadfast love, would keep
        Your watch around us while we sleep.

        From evil dreams defend our sight,
        From fears and terrors of the night;
        Tread underfoot our deadly foe
        That we no sinful thought may know.

        O Father, that we ask be done
        Through Jesus Christ, your only Son;
        And Holy Spirit, by whose breath
        Our souls are raised to life from death.

The Word of God

Psalmody

One or more of the following psalms may be used (a diamond at the end of a line indicates a brief pause):

Psalm 4

1   Answer me when I call, O God of my righteousness; ◆
     you set me at liberty when I was in trouble;
         have mercy on me and hear my prayer.

2   How long will you nobles dishonour my glory; ♦
how long will you love vain things and seek after falsehood?

3   But know that the Lord has shown me
      his marvellous kindness; ♦
when I call upon the Lord, he will hear me.

4   Stand in awe, and sin not; ♦
commune with your own heart upon your bed, and be still.

5   Offer the sacrifices of righteousness ♦
and put your trust in the Lord.

6   There are many that say, 'Who will show us any good?' ♦
Lord, lift up the light of your countenance upon us.

7   You have put gladness in my heart, ♦
more than when their corn and wine and oil increase.

8   In peace I will lie down and sleep, ♦
for it is you Lord, only, who make me dwell in safety.

Psalm 91

1   Whoever dwells in the shelter of the Most High ♦
and abides under the shadow of the Almighty,

2   Shall say to the Lord, 'My refuge and my stronghold, ♦
my God, in whom I put my trust.'

3   For he shall deliver you from the snare of the fowler ♦
and from the deadly pestilence.

4   He shall cover you with his wings
      and you shall be safe under his feathers; ♦
his faithfulness shall be your shield and buckler.

5   You shall not be afraid of any terror by night, ♦
nor of the arrow that flies by day;

6   Of the pestilence that stalks in darkness, ◆
    nor of the sickness that destroys at noonday.

7   Though a thousand fall at your side
        and ten thousand at your right hand, ◆
    yet it shall not come near you.

8   Your eyes have only to behold ◆
    to see the reward of the wicked.

9   Because you have made the Lord your refuge ◆
    and the Most High your stronghold,

10 There shall no evil happen to you, ◆
    neither shall any plague come near your tent.

11 For he shall give his angels charge over you, ◆
    to keep you in all your ways.

12 They shall bear you in their hands, ◆
    lest you dash your foot against a stone.

13 You shall tread upon the lion and adder; ◆
    the young lion and the serpent you shall trample underfoot.

14 Because they have set their love upon me,
        therefore will I deliver them; ◆
    I will lift them up, because they know my name.

15 They will call upon me and I will answer them; ◆
    I am with them in trouble,
        I will deliver them and bring them to honour.

16 With long life will I satisfy them ◆
    and show them my salvation.

1   Come, bless the Lord, all you servants of the Lord, ◆
      you that by night stand in the house of the Lord.

2   Lift up your hands towards the sanctuary ◆
      and bless the Lord.

3   The Lord who made heaven and earth ◆
      give you blessing out of Zion.

At the end of the psalmody, the following is said or sung:

Glory to the Father and to the Son
and to the Holy Spirit;
as it was in the beginning is now
and shall be for ever.
Amen.

Scripture Reading

One of the following short lessons or another suitable passage is read:

You, O Lord, are in the midst of us and we are called by your name; leave us not, O Lord our God. (Jeremiah 14.9)

or

Be sober, be vigilant, because your adversary the devil is prowling round like a roaring lion, seeking for someone to devour. Resist him, strong in the faith. (1 Peter 5.8, 9)

or

The servants of the Lamb shall see the face of God, whose name will be on their foreheads. There will be no more night: they will not need the light of a lamp or the light of the sun, for God will be their light, and they will reign for ever and ever. (Revelation 22.4, 5)

The following responsory may be said:

Into your hands, O Lord, I commend my spirit.
All **Into your hands, O Lord, I commend my spirit.**
For you have redeemed me, Lord God of truth.
All **I commend my spirit.**
Glory to the Father and to the Son, and to the Holy Spirit.
All **Into your hands, O Lord, I commend my spirit.**

Or, in Easter:

Into your hands, O Lord, I commend my spirit.
    Alleluia, alleluia.
All **Into your hands, O Lord, I commend my spirit.**
    Alleluia, alleluia.
For you have redeemed me, Lord God of truth.
All **Alleluia, alleluia.**
Glory to the Father and to the Son, and to the Holy Spirit.
All **Into your hands, O Lord, I commend my spirit.**
    Alleluia, alleluia.

Keep me as the apple of your eye.
All **Hide me under the shadow of your wings.**

The Nunc dimittis (The Song of Simeon) is said or sung.

All **Save us, O Lord, while waking,**
and guard us while sleeping,
that awake we may watch with Christ
and asleep may rest in peace.

1 Now, Lord, you let your servant go in peace: ♦
your word has been fulfilled.

2 My own eyes have seen the salvation ♦
which you have prepared in the sight of every people;

3 A light to reveal you to the nations ♦
and the glory of your people Israel. (Luke 2.29–32)

Glory to the Father and to the Son
and to the Holy Spirit;
as it was in the beginning is now
and shall be for ever. Amen.

All **Save us, O Lord, while waking,**
and guard us while sleeping,
that awake we may watch with Christ
and asleep may rest in peace.

Prayers

Intercessions and thanksgivings may be offered here.

Silence may be kept.

Visit this place, O Lord, we pray,
and drive far from it the snares of the enemy;
may your holy angels dwell with us and guard us in peace,
and may your blessing be always upon us;
through Jesus Christ our Lord.

All   **Amen.**

The Lord's Prayer may be said.

The Conclusion

In peace we will lie down and sleep;
All   **for you alone, Lord, make us dwell in safety.**

Abide with us, Lord Jesus,
All   **for the night is at hand and the day is now past.**

As the night watch looks for the morning,
All   **so do we look for you, O Christ.**

[Come with the dawning of the day
All   **and make yourself known in the breaking of the bread.**]

The Lord bless us and watch over us;
the Lord make his face shine upon us and be gracious to us;
the Lord look kindly on us and give us peace.

All   **Amen.**

PSALMS FOR SUNDAYS AND FESTIVALS

The space given to the Psalms in our worship shows just how important they are to Christian worship and in particular to Anglican liturgy. The Psalms (or the Psalter) has always had a special place in the worship of the Church of England, giving colour and light to Morning and Evening Prayer and finding echoes in our own enthusiasm for hymnody. Saying or singing the Psalms is not about repetition but about recitation, reciting the poetry of worship that has been offered in praise of God down the ages. The Psalms give us a vocabulary of heaven.

STRUCTURE

Most of the Psalms were probably composed to accompany acts of worship and can be classified in this way:

* *Hymns* – acts of praise for general and specific occasions;
* *Laments* – seeking deliverance for the individual or the community;
* *Songs of Trust* – placing confidence in God's activity;
* *Thanksgivings* – expressions of gratitude;
* *History* – recalling God's involvement in human experience;
* *Royal Psalms* – to be used on formal, civic worship occasions;
* *Wisdom Psalms* – meditations on God himself;
* *Liturgies* – songs for worship occasions.

The Psalms come from many different sources but have traditionally been attributed to King David, a hymn writer and singer and King of Israel.

SHAPE

In the Christian Church the Psalms have been used in many ways. Among the early Christians, they were recited and sung as links with their heritage and as well-known expressions of community worship. In the Middle Ages, the monastic tradition made the recitation of the Psalter the framework for the consecration and ordering of time. Since then, the Psalms have been widely used in eucharistic worship and have greatly influenced the writing of hymns.

The *Common Worship* Psalter has been prepared to complement all *Common Worship* services. It uses the 'you' form of language. It is scholarly, being faithful to its Hebrew origins. The psalms in *Common Worship* may be said or sung as the worship occasion requires. A small diamond at the end of the line indicates a brief pause.

SPIRIT

The living spirit of any worshipping community can be found in its hymns. The Christian community has always valued the Psalms as a common expression of faith in God. The Psalms provide, both for individual prayer and for the prayer of the whole community, a treasury of words when, as so often, our own words are not enough. The Psalms belong to us all and help us worship the God who is yesterday, today and for ever. The Psalms used on Sundays and Festivals are included in this book, together with a calendar, so that people may be able to pray the psalm of the week, or prepare for the coming Sunday by praying the appointed psalm.

PSALMS FOR SUNDAYS
AND FESTIVALS

Year A begins at Advent in 2010, 2013, 2016, 2019
Year B begins at Advent in 2008, 2011, 2014, 2017
Year C begins at Advent in 2009, 2012, 2015, 2018

After Trinity Sunday the Psalm given is for the Sunday which falls within the two dates.

	Year A	Year B	Year C
Advent 1	Ps. 122	Ps. 80.1–7, 16–18	Ps. 25.1–10
Advent 2	Ps. 72.1–7, 18–19	Ps. 85.1–2, 8–13	Benedictus, see p. 296
Advent 3	Ps. 146.4–9	Ps. 126	Isaiah 12.2–6, see p. 297
Advent 4	Ps. 80 1–7, 16–18	Ps. 89.1–4, 19–26	Magnificat, see p. 298
Christmas	(set 1) Ps. 96	See A	See A
	(set 2) Ps. 97	See A	See A
	(set 3) Ps. 98	See A	See A
Christmas 1	Ps. 148	Ps. 148	Ps. 148
Christmas 2	Ps. 147.143–21	See A	See A
Epiphany	Ps. 72.1–7, 10–14	See A	See A
Baptism of Christ	Ps. 29	Ps. 29	Ps. 29
Epiphany 2	Ps. 40.1–11	Ps. 139.1–5, 12–17	Ps. 36.5–10
Epiphany 3	Ps. 27.1, 5–13	Ps. 128	Ps. 19
Epiphany 4	Ps. 36.5–10	Ps. 111	Ps. 48
Presentation	Ps. 24.1–6, 7–10	See A	See A
4–10 February	Ps. 112.1–9, 10	Ps. 147.1–12, 20c	Ps. 138
11–16 February	Ps. 119.1–8	Ps. 30	Ps. 1
18–24 February	Ps. 119.33–40	Ps. 41	Ps. 37. 1–12, 41–42
2 before Lent	Ps. 136.1–9, 10–22, 23–26,	Ps. 104.26–37	Ps. 65
Next before Lent	Ps. 2 or 99	Ps. 50.1–6	Ps. 99

	Year A	Year B	Year C
Ash Wednesday	Ps. 51.1–18	See A	See A
Lent 1	Ps. 32	Ps. 25.1–10	Ps. 91.1–2, 9–16
Lent 2	Ps. 121	Ps. 22.22–30	Ps. 27
Lent 3	Ps. 95	Ps. 19	Ps. 63.1–8
Lent 4	Ps. 23	Ps. 107.1–3, 17–22	Ps. 32
Mothering	Ps. 34.11–20 or 127.1–4	See A	See A
Lent 5	Ps. 130	Ps. 51.1–12	Ps. 126
Palm Sunday	Ps. 118.1–2, 19–29 Ps. 31.9–16	See A	See A
Maundy Thursday	Ps. 116.1, 10–17	See A	See A
Good Friday	Ps. 22	See A	See A
Easter Day	Ps. 118.1–2, 14–24	See A	See A
Easter 2	Ps. 16	Ps. 133	Ps. 118.14–29 or 150
Easter 3	Ps. 116.1–3, 10–17	Ps. 4	Ps. 30
Easter 4	Ps. 23	Ps. 23	Ps. 23
Easter 5	Ps. 31. 1–5, 15–16	Ps. 22.24–30	Ps. 148
Easter 6	Ps. 66. 7–18	Ps. 98	Ps. 67
Ascension	Ps. 110, 150	See A	See A
Easter 7	Ps. 68.1–10, 33–36	Ps. 1	Ps. 97
Pentecost	Ps. 104.25–35, 37	Ps. 104. 25–35, 37	Ps. 104.25–35, 37
Trinity	Ps. 8	Ps. 29	Ps. 8
Corpus Christi	Ps. 116.10–17	See A	See A
24–28 May	Ps. 119.33–40	Ps. 41	Ps. 37.1–12, 41–42
29 May–4 June	Ps. 46 or 31.1–5, 19–24	Ps. 139. 1–5, 12–17	Ps. 96
5–11 June	Ps. 33.1–12 or 50.7–15	Ps. 138 or 130 or 81.1–10	Ps. 146 or 30
12–18 June	Ps. 116.1, 10–17	Ps. 20 or 92.1–4, 11–14	Ps. 5.1–8 or 32
19–25 June	Ps. 86.1–10, 16–17 or 69.8–20	Ps. 9.9–20 or 133	Ps. 42 and 43 or 22.18–27
26 June–2 July	Ps. 13 or 89.1–4, 15–18	Ps. 130 or 30	Ps. 77. 1–2, 11–20 or 16
3–9 July	Ps. 45.11–18 or 145.8–15	Ps. 48 or 123	Ps. 30 or 66.1–8
10–16 July	Ps. 119.105–112 or 65.1–13	Ps. 24 or 85. 8–13	Ps. 82 or 25.1–10

	Year A	Year B	Year C
17–23 July	Ps. 139.1–11, 22–23 or 86.11–17	Ps. 89.20–37 or 23	Ps. 52 or 15
24–30 July	Ps. 105.1–11, 45b or 119.129–136	Ps. 14 or 145.10–19	Ps. 85 or 138
31 July–6 August	Ps. 17.1–7, 16 or 145.8–9, 15–22	Ps. 51.1–12 or 78.23–29	Ps. 107. 1–16, 43 or 49. 1–12
7–13 August	Ps. 105.1–6, 16–22.45b or 85.8–13	Ps. 130 or 34.1–8	Ps. 50.1–8, 3–24 or 33.12–21
14–20 August	Ps. 133 or 67	Ps. 111 or 34.9–14	Ps. 80.1–2, 8–18 or 82
21–27 August	Ps. 124 or 138	Ps. 84 or 34.15–22	Ps. 71.1–6 or 103.1–8
28 August– 3 September	Ps. 105.1–6, 23–26, 45b or 26.1–8	Ps. 45.1–2, 7–10 or 15	Ps. 81.1, 10–16 or 112
4–10 September	Ps. 149 or 119.33–40	Ps. 125 or 146	Ps. 139. 1–5, 12–17 or 1
11–17 September	Ps. 114 or 103.1–13	Ps. 19 or 116.1–8	Ps. 14 or 51.1–10
18–24 September	Ps. 105.1–6, 37–45 or 145.1–8	Ps. 1 or 54	Ps. 79. 1–9 or 113
25 September– 1 October	Ps. 78.1–4, 12–16 or 25.1–10	Ps. 124 or 19.7–14	Ps. 91.1–6, 14–16 or 146
2–8 October	Ps. 80.9–17	Ps. 26 or 8	Ps. 137 or 37.1–10
9–15 October	Ps. 106.1–6, 19–23 or 23	Ps. 22.1–15 or 90.13–17	Ps. 66. 1–11 or 111
16–22 October	Ps. 96.1–13	Ps. 104.1–9, 25.37b or 91.9–16	Ps. 119.97–104 or 121
23–29 October	Ps. 90.1–6, 13–17 or 1	Ps. 34.1–8, 19–22 or 126	Ps. 65 or 84.1–7
Bible Sunday	Ps. 119.9–16	Ps. 19.7–14	Ps. 119.129–136
Dedication	Ps. 122	See A	See A
4 before Advent	Ps. 107.1–9, 33–37 or 43	Ps. 146 or 119.1–8	Ps. 32.1–8
All Saints'	Ps. 34.1–10	Ps. 24.1–6	Ps. 149
3 before Advent	Ps. 78.1–7 or 70	Ps. 62.6–14	Ps. 17.1–9
2 before Advent	Ps. 90.1–12	Ps. 16	Ps. 98
Christ the King	Ps. 95.1–7	Ps. 132.1–19	Ps. 46

Psalms

1   Blessed are they who have not walked
        in the counsel of the wicked, ◆
    nor lingered in the way of sinners,
        nor sat in the assembly of the scornful.

2   Their delight is in the law of the Lord ◆
    and they meditate on his law day and night.

3   Like a tree planted by streams of water
        bearing fruit in due season, with leaves that do not wither, ◆
    whatever they do, it shall prosper.

4   As for the wicked, it is not so with them; ◆
    they are like chaff which the wind blows away.

5   Therefore the wicked shall not be able to stand
        in the judgement, ◆
    nor the sinner in the congregation of the righteous.

6   For the Lord knows the way of the righteous, ◆
    but the way of the wicked shall perish.

Psalm 2

1   Why are the nations in tumult, ◆
    and why do the peoples devise a vain plot?

2   The kings of the earth rise up,
        and the rulers take counsel together, ◆
    against the Lord and against his anointed:

3   'Let us break their bonds asunder ◆
    and cast away their cords from us.'

4   He who dwells in heaven shall laugh them to scorn; ◆
    the Lord shall have them in derision.

5   Then shall he speak to them in his wrath ◆
    and terrify them in his fury:

6   'Yet have I set my king ◆
    upon my holy hill of Zion.'

7   I will proclaim the decree of the Lord; ◆
    he said to me: 'You are my Son; this day have I begotten you.

8   'Ask of me and I will give you the nations for your inheritance ◆
    and the ends of the earth for your possession.

9   'You shall break them with a rod of iron ◆
     and dash them in pieces like a potter's vessel.'

10   Now therefore be wise, O kings; ◆
     be prudent, you judges of the earth.
11   Serve the Lord with fear, and with trembling kiss his feet, ◆
     lest he be angry and you perish from the way,
         for his wrath is quickly kindled.
12   Happy are all they ◆
     who take refuge in him.

Psalm 4

1   Answer me when I call, O God of my righteousness; ◆
     you set me at liberty when I was in trouble;
         have mercy on me and hear my prayer.
2   How long will you nobles dishonour my glory; ◆
     how long will you love vain things and seek after falsehood?
3   But know that the Lord has shown me his marvellous kindness; ◆
     when I call upon the Lord, he will hear me.
4   Stand in awe, and sin not; ◆
     commune with your own heart upon your bed, and be still.
5   Offer the sacrifices of righteousness ◆
     and put your trust in the Lord.
6   There are many that say, 'Who will show us any good?' ◆
     Lord, lift up the light of your countenance upon us.
7   You have put gladness in my heart, ◆
     more than when their corn and wine and oil increase.
8   In peace I will lie down and sleep, ◆
     for it is you Lord, only, who make me dwell in safety.

Psalm 5

1   Give ear to my words, O Lord; ◆
     consider my lamentation.
2   Hearken to the voice of my crying, my King and my God, ◆
     for to you I make my prayer.
3   In the morning, Lord, you will hear my voice; ◆
     early in the morning I make my appeal to you, and look up.
4   For you are the God who takes no pleasure in wickedness; ◆
     no evil can dwell with you.

5   The boastful cannot stand in your sight; ◆
      you hate all those that work wickedness.
6   You destroy those who speak lies; ◆
      the bloodthirsty and deceitful the Lord will abhor.
7   But as for me, through the greatness of your mercy,
          I will come into your house; ◆
      I will bow down towards your holy temple in awe of you.
8   Lead me, Lord, in your righteousness,
          because of my enemies; ◆
      make your way straight before my face.

Psalm 8

First version

1   *O Lord our governor,* ◆
      how glorious is your name in all the world!
2   Your majesty above the heavens is praised ◆
      out of the mouths of babes at the breast.
3   You have founded a stronghold against your foes, ◆
      that you might still the enemy and the avenger.

4   When I consider your heavens, the work of your fingers, ◆
      the moon and the stars that you have ordained,
5   What is man, that you should be mindful of him; ◆
      the son of man, that you should seek him out?
6   You have made him little lower than the angels ◆
      and crown him with glory and honour.
7   You have given him dominion over the works of your hands ◆
      and put all things under his feet.

Second version

1   *O Lord our governor,* ◆
      how glorious is your name in all the world!
2   Your majesty above the heavens is praised ◆
      out of the mouths of babes at the breast.
3   You have founded a stronghold against your foes, ◆
      that you might still the enemy and the avenger.

4   When I consider your heavens, the work of your fingers, ♦
the moon and the stars that you have ordained,

5   What are mortals, that you should be mindful of them; ♦
mere human beings, that you should seek them out?

6   You have made them little lower than the angels ♦
and crown them with glory and honour.

7   You have given them dominion over the works of your hands ♦
and put all things under their feet,

8   All sheep and oxen, ♦
even the wild beasts of the field,

9   The birds of the air, the fish of the sea ♦
and whatsoever moves in the paths of the sea.

10   *O Lord our governor,* ♦
how glorious is your name in all the world!

Psalm 9

9   Then will the Lord be a refuge for the oppressed, ♦
a refuge in the time of trouble.

10   And those who know your name will put their trust in you, ♦
for you, Lord, have never failed those who seek you.

11   Sing praises to the Lord who dwells in Zion; ♦
declare among the peoples the things he has done.

12   The avenger of blood has remembered them; ♦
he did not forget the cry of the oppressed.

13   Have mercy upon me, O Lord; ♦
consider the trouble I suffer from those who hate me,
    you that lift me up from the gates of death;

14   That I may tell all your praises in the gates of the city of Zion ♦
and rejoice in your salvation.

15   The nations shall sink into the pit of their making ♦
and in the snare which they set will their own foot be taken.

16   The Lord makes himself known by his acts of justice; ♦
the wicked are snared in the works of their own hands.

17   They shall return to the land of darkness, ♦
all the nations that forget God.

18   For the needy shall not always be forgotten ♦
and the hope of the poor shall not perish for ever.

19 Arise, O Lord, and let not mortals have the upper hand; ◆
let the nations be judged before your face.
20 Put them in fear, O Lord, ◆
that the nations may know themselves to be but mortal.

Psalm 13

1 How long will you forget me, O Lord; for ever? ◆
How long will you hide your face from me?
2 How long shall I have anguish in my soul
and grief in my heart, day after day? ◆
How long shall my enemy triumph over me?
3 Look upon me and answer, O Lord my God; ◆
lighten my eyes, lest I sleep in death;
4 Lest my enemy say, 'I have prevailed against him,' ◆
and my foes rejoice that I have fallen.

5 But I put my trust in your steadfast love; ◆
my heart will rejoice in your salvation.
6 I will sing to the Lord, ◆
for he has dealt so bountifully with me.

Psalm 14

1 The fool has said in his heart, 'There is no God.' ◆
Corrupt are they, and abominable in their wickedness;
there is no one that does good.
2 The Lord has looked down from heaven
upon the children of earth, ◆
to see if there is anyone who is wise
and seeks after God.
3 But every one has turned back;
all alike have become corrupt: ◆
there is none that does good; no, not one.
4 Have they no knowledge, those evildoers, ◆
who eat up my people as if they ate bread
and do not call upon the Lord?
5 There shall they be in great fear; ◆
for God is in the company of the righteous.
6 Though they would confound the counsel of the poor, ◆
yet the Lord shall be their refuge.

7   O that Israel's salvation would come out of Zion! ♦
     When the Lord restores the fortunes of his people,
         then will Jacob rejoice and Israel be glad.

Psalm 15

1   Lord, who may dwell in your tabernacle? ♦
     Who may rest upon your holy hill?
2   Whoever leads an uncorrupt life ♦
     and does the thing that is right;
3   Who speaks the truth from the heart ♦
     and bears no deceit on the tongue;
4   Who does no evil to a friend ♦
     and pours no scorn on a neighbour;
5   In whose sight the wicked are not esteemed, ♦
     but who honours those who fear the Lord.
6   Whoever has sworn to a neighbour ♦
     and never goes back on that word;
7   Who does not lend money in hope of gain, ♦
     nor takes a bribe against the innocent;
8   Whoever does these things ♦
     shall never fall.

Psalm 16

1   Preserve me, O God, for in you have I taken refuge; ♦
     I have said to the Lord, 'You are my lord,
         all my good depends on you.'
2   All my delight is upon the godly that are in the land, ♦
     upon those who are noble in heart.
3   Though the idols are legion
     that many run after, ♦
     their drink offerings of blood I will not offer,
     neither make mention of their names upon my lips.
4   The Lord himself is my portion and my cup; ♦
     in your hands alone is my fortune.
5   My share has fallen in a fair land; ♦
     indeed, I have a goodly heritage.

6   I will bless the Lord who has given me counsel, ♦
     and in the night watches he instructs my heart.

7   I have set the Lord always before me; ◆
he is at my right hand; I shall not fall.

8   Wherefore my heart is glad and my spirit rejoices; ◆
my flesh also shall rest secure.

9   For you will not abandon my soul to Death, ◆
nor suffer your faithful one to see the Pit.

10   You will show me the path of life;
      in your presence is the fullness of joy ◆
and in your right hand are pleasures for evermore.

Psalm 17

1   Hear my just cause, O Lord; consider my complaint; ◆
listen to my prayer, which comes not from lying lips.

2   Let my vindication come forth from your presence; ◆
let your eyes behold what is right.

3   Weigh my heart, examine me by night, ◆
refine me, and you will find no impurity in me.

4   My mouth does not trespass for earthly rewards; ◆
I have heeded the words of your lips.

5   My footsteps hold fast in the ways of your commandments; ◆
my feet have not stumbled in your paths.

6   I call upon you, O God, for you will answer me; ◆
incline your ear to me, and listen to my words.

7   Show me your marvellous loving-kindness, ◆
O Saviour of those who take refuge at your right hand
      from those who rise up against them.

8   Keep me as the apple of your eye; ◆
hide me under the shadow of your wings,

16   As for me, I shall see your face in righteousness; ◆
when I awake and behold your likeness, I shall be satisfied.

Psalm 19

1   The heavens are telling the glory of God ◆
and the firmament proclaims his handiwork.

2   One day pours out its song to another ◆
and one night unfolds knowledge to another.

3   They have neither speech nor language ◆
and their voices are not heard,

4   Yet their sound has gone out into all lands ◆
      and their words to the ends of the world.
5   In them has he set a tabernacle for the sun, ◆
      that comes forth as a bridegroom out of his chamber
         and rejoices as a champion to run his course.
6   It goes forth from the end of the heavens
         and runs to the very end again, ◆
      and there is nothing hidden from its heat.

7   The law of the Lord is perfect, reviving the soul; ◆
      the testimony of the Lord is sure
         and gives wisdom to the simple.
8   The statutes of the Lord are right and rejoice the heart; ◆
      the commandment of the Lord is pure
         and gives light to the eyes.
9   The fear of the Lord is clean and endures for ever; ◆
      the judgements of the Lord are true
         and righteous altogether.
10   More to be desired are they than gold,
         more than much fine gold, ◆
      sweeter also than honey,
         dripping from the honeycomb.
11   By them also is your servant taught ◆
      and in keeping them there is great reward.

12   Who can tell how often they offend? ◆
      O cleanse me from my secret faults!
13   Keep your servant also from presumptuous sins
         lest they get dominion over me; ◆
      so shall I be undefiled,
         and innocent of great offence.
14   Let the words of my mouth and the meditation of my heart
         be acceptable in your sight, ◆
      O Lord, my strength and my redeemer.

Psalm 20

1   May the Lord hear you in the day of trouble, ◆
      the name of the God of Jacob defend you;

2   Send you help from his sanctuary ◆
and strengthen you out of Zion;
3   Remember all your offerings ◆
and accept your burnt sacrifice;
4   Grant you your heart's desire ◆
and fulfil all your mind.
5   May we rejoice in your salvation
    and triumph in the name of our God; ◆
may the Lord perform all your petitions.

6   Now I know that the Lord will save his anointed; ◆
he will answer him from his holy heaven,
    with the mighty strength of his right hand.
7   Some put their trust in chariots and some in horses, ◆
but we will call only on the name of the Lord our God.
8   They are brought down and fallen, ◆
but we are risen and stand upright.
9   O Lord, save the king ◆
and answer us when we call upon you.

Psalm 22

1   My God, my God, why have you forsaken me, ◆
and are so far from my salvation,
    from the words of my distress?
2   O my God, I cry in the daytime,
    but you do not answer; ◆
and by night also, but I find no rest.
3   Yet you are the Holy One, ◆
enthroned upon the praises of Israel.
4   Our forebears trusted in you; ◆
they trusted, and you delivered them.
5   They cried out to you and were delivered; ◆
they put their trust in you and were not confounded.
6   But as for me, I am a worm and no man, ◆
scorned by all and despised by the people.
7   All who see me laugh me to scorn; ◆
they curl their lips and wag their heads, saying,
8   'He trusted in the Lord; let him deliver him; ◆
let him deliver him, if he delights in him.'

9   But it is you that took me out of the womb ◆
    and laid me safe upon my mother's breast.
10 On you was I cast ever since I was born; ◆
    you are my God even from my mother's womb.
11 Be not far from me, for trouble is near at hand ◆
    and there is none to help.
12 Mighty oxen come around me; ◆
    fat bulls of Bashan close me in on every side.
13 They gape upon me with their mouths, ◆
    as it were a ramping and a roaring lion.
14 I am poured out like water;
        all my bones are out of joint; ◆
    my heart has become like wax
        melting in the depths of my body.
15 My mouth is dried up like a potsherd;
        my tongue cleaves to my gums; ◆
    you have laid me in the dust of death.
16 For the hounds are all about me,
        the pack of evildoers close in on me; ◆
    they pierce my hands and my feet.
17 I can count all my bones; ◆
    they stand staring and looking upon me.
18 They divide my garments among them; ◆
    they cast lots for my clothing.
19 Be not far from me, O Lord; ◆
    you are my strength; hasten to help me.
20 Deliver my soul from the sword, ◆
    my poor life from the power of the dog.
21 Save me from the lion's mouth,
        from the horns of wild oxen. ◆
    You have answered me!

22 I will tell of your name to my people; ◆
    in the midst of the congregation will I praise you.
23 Praise the Lord, you that fear him; ◆
    O seed of Jacob, glorify him;
        stand in awe of him, O seed of Israel.
24 For he has not despised nor abhorred the suffering of the poor;
        neither has he hidden his face from them; ◆
    but when they cried to him he heard them.

25 From you comes my praise in the great congregation; ◆
I will perform my vows
   in the presence of those that fear you.
26 The poor shall eat and be satisfied; ◆
those who seek the Lord shall praise him;
   their hearts shall live for ever.

27 All the ends of the earth
   shall remember and turn to the Lord, ◆
and all the families of the nations shall bow before him.
28 For the kingdom is the Lord's ◆
and he rules over the nations.
29 How can those who sleep in the earth
   bow down in worship, ◆
or those who go down to the dust kneel before him?
30 He has saved my life for himself;
   my descendants shall serve him; ◆
this shall be told of the Lord for generations to come.
31 They shall come and make known his salvation,
   to a people yet unborn, ◆
declaring that he, the Lord, has done it.

Psalm 23

1 The Lord is my shepherd; ◆
therefore can I lack nothing.
2 He makes me lie down in green pastures ◆
and leads me beside still waters.
3 He shall refresh my soul ◆
and guide me in the paths of righteousness for his name's sake.
4 Though I walk through the valley of the shadow of death,
   I will fear no evil; ◆
for you are with me;
   your rod and your staff, they comfort me.
5 You spread a table before me
   in the presence of those who trouble me; ◆
you have anointed my head with oil
   and my cup shall be full.

6   Surely goodness and loving mercy shall follow me
       all the days of my life, ◆
     and I will dwell in the house of the Lord for ever.

Psalm 24

1   The earth is the Lord's and all that fills it, ◆
     the compass of the world and all who dwell therein.
2   For he has founded it upon the seas ◆
     and set it firm upon the rivers of the deep.

3   'Who shall ascend the hill of the Lord, ◆
     or who can rise up in his holy place?'
4   'Those who have clean hands and a pure heart, ◆
     who have not lifted up their soul to an idol,
       nor sworn an oath to a lie;
5   'They shall receive a blessing from the Lord, ◆
     a just reward from the God of their salvation.'
6   Such is the company of those who seek him, ◆
     of those who seek your face, O God of Jacob.

7   Lift up your heads, O gates;
       be lifted up, you everlasting doors; ◆
     and the King of glory shall come in.
8   'Who is the King of glory?' ◆
     'The Lord, strong and mighty,
       the Lord who is mighty in battle.'
9   Lift up your heads, O gates;
       be lifted up, you everlasting doors; ◆
     and the King of glory shall come in.
10   'Who is this King of glory?' ◆
     'The Lord of hosts,
       he is the King of glory.'

Psalm 25

1   To you, O Lord, I lift up my soul;
       O my God, in you I trust; ◆
     let me not be put to shame;
       let not my enemies triumph over me.

2   Let none who look to you be put to shame, ♦
     but let the treacherous be shamed and frustrated.
3   Make me to know your ways, O Lord, ♦
     and teach me your paths.
4   Lead me in your truth and teach me, ♦
     for you are the God of my salvation;
         for you have I hoped all the day long.
5   Remember, Lord, your compassion and love, ♦
     for they are from everlasting.
6   Remember not the sins of my youth
         or my transgressions, ♦
     but think on me in your goodness, O Lord,
         according to your steadfast love.
7   Gracious and upright is the Lord; ♦
     therefore shall he teach sinners in the way.
8   He will guide the humble in doing right ♦
     and teach his way to the lowly.
9   All the paths of the Lord are mercy and truth ♦
     to those who keep his covenant and his testimonies.
10   For your name's sake, O Lord, ♦
     be merciful to my sin, for it is great.

Psalm 26

1   Give judgement for me, O Lord,
         for I have walked with integrity; ♦
     I have trusted in the Lord and have not faltered.
2   Test me, O Lord, and try me; ♦
     examine my heart and my mind.
3   For your love is before my eyes; ♦
     I have walked in your truth.
4   I have not joined the company of the false, ♦
     nor consorted with the deceitful.
5   I hate the gathering of evildoers ♦
     and I will not sit down with the wicked.
6   I will wash my hands in innocence, O Lord, ♦
     that I may go about your altar,
7   To make heard the voice of thanksgiving ♦
     and tell of all your wonderful deeds.

8   Lord, I love the house of your habitation ♦
     and the place where your glory abides.

9   Sweep me not away with sinners, ♦
     nor my life with the bloodthirsty,

10   Whose hands are full of wicked schemes ♦
     and their right hand full of bribes.

11   As for me, I will walk with integrity; ♦
     redeem me, Lord, and be merciful to me.

12   My foot stands firm; ♦
     in the great congregation I will bless the Lord.

Psalm 27

1   The Lord is my light and my salvation;
     whom then shall I fear? ♦
    The Lord is the strength of my life;
     of whom then shall I be afraid?

2   When the wicked, even my enemies and my foes,
     came upon me to eat up my flesh, ♦
    they stumbled and fell.

3   Though a host encamp against me,
     my heart shall not be afraid, ♦
    and though there rise up war against me,
     yet will I put my trust in him.

4   One thing have I asked of the Lord
     and that alone I seek: ♦
    that I may dwell in the house of the Lord
     all the days of my life,

5   To behold the fair beauty of the Lord ♦
     and to seek his will in his temple.

6   For in the day of trouble
     he shall hide me in his shelter; ♦
    in the secret place of his dwelling shall he hide me
     and set me high upon a rock.

7   And now shall he lift up my head ♦
     above my enemies round about me;

8   Therefore will I offer in his dwelling an oblation
     with great gladness; ♦
    I will sing and make music to the Lord.

9   Hear my voice, O Lord, when I call; ◆
    have mercy upon me and answer me.
10 My heart tells of your word, 'Seek my face.' ◆
    Your face, Lord, will I seek.
11 Hide not your face from me, ◆
    nor cast your servant away in displeasure.
12 You have been my helper; ◆
    leave me not, neither forsake me, O God of my salvation.
13 Though my father and my mother forsake me, ◆
    the Lord will take me up.
14 Teach me your way, O Lord; ◆
    lead me on a level path,
        because of those who lie in wait for me.
15 Deliver me not into the will of my adversaries, ◆
    for false witnesses have risen up against me,
        and those who breathe out violence.
16 I believe that I shall see the goodness of the Lord ◆
    in the land of the living.
17 Wait for the Lord;
        be strong and he shall comfort your heart; ◆
    wait patiently for the Lord.

Psalm 29

1   Ascribe to the Lord, you powers of heaven, ◆
    ascribe to the Lord glory and strength.
2   Ascribe to the Lord the honour due to his name; ◆
    worship the Lord in the beauty of holiness.
3   The voice of the Lord is upon the waters;
        the God of glory thunders; ◆
    the Lord is upon the mighty waters.
4   The voice of the Lord is mighty in operation; ◆
    the voice of the Lord is a glorious voice.
5   The voice of the Lord breaks the cedar trees; ◆
    the Lord breaks the cedars of Lebanon;
6   He makes Lebanon skip like a calf ◆
    and Sirion like a young wild ox.
7   The voice of the Lord splits the flash of lightning;
        the voice of the Lord shakes the wilderness; ◆
    the Lord shakes the wilderness of Kadesh.

8   The voice of the Lord makes the oak trees writhe
        and strips the forests bare; ◆
    in his temple all cry, 'Glory!'

9   The Lord sits enthroned above the water flood; ◆
    the Lord sits enthroned as king for evermore.

10   The Lord shall give strength to his people; ◆
    the Lord shall give his people the blessing of peace.

Psalm 30

1   I will exalt you, O Lord,
        because you have raised me up ◆
    and have not let my foes triumph over me.

2   O Lord my God, I cried out to you ◆
    and you have healed me.

3   You brought me up, O Lord, from the dead; ◆
    you restored me to life from among those that go down to the Pit.

4   Sing to the Lord, you servants of his; ◆
    give thanks to his holy name.

5   For his wrath endures but the twinkling of an eye,
        his favour for a lifetime. ◆
    Heaviness may endure for a night,
        but joy comes in the morning.

6   In my prosperity I said,
        'I shall never be moved. ◆
    You, Lord, of your goodness,
        have made my hill so strong.'

7   Then you hid your face from me ◆
    and I was utterly dismayed.

8   To you, O Lord, I cried; ◆
    to the Lord I made my supplication:

9   'What profit is there in my blood,
        if I go down to the Pit? ◆
    Will the dust praise you or declare your faithfulness?

10   'Hear, O Lord, and have mercy upon me; ◆
    O Lord, be my helper.'

11   You have turned my mourning into dancing; ◆
    you have put off my sackcloth and girded me with gladness;

12　　Therefore my heart sings to you without ceasing; ◆
　　　O Lord my God, I will give you thanks for ever.

1　　In you, O Lord, have I taken refuge;
　　　　let me never be put to shame; ◆
　　　deliver me in your righteousness.
2　　Incline your ear to me; ◆
　　　make haste to deliver me.
3　　Be my strong rock, a fortress to save me,
　　　　for you are my rock and my stronghold; ◆
　　　guide me, and lead me for your name's sake.
4　　Take me out of the net
　　　　that they have laid secretly for me, ◆
　　　for you are my strength.
5　　Into your hands I commend my spirit, ◆
　　　for you have redeemed me, O Lord God of truth.
6　　I hate those who cling to worthless idols; ◆
　　　I put my trust in the Lord.

9　　Have mercy on me, Lord, for I am in trouble; ◆
　　　my eye is consumed with sorrow,
　　　　my soul and my body also.
10　For my life is wasted with grief,
　　　　and my years with sighing; ◆
　　　my strength fails me because of my affliction,
　　　　and my bones are consumed.
11　I have become a reproach to all my enemies
　　　　and even to my neighbours,
　　　　　an object of dread to my acquaintances; ◆
　　　when they see me in the street they flee from me.
12　I am forgotten like one that is dead, out of mind; ◆
　　　I have become like a broken vessel.
13　For I have heard the whispering of the crowd;
　　　　fear is on every side; ◆
　　　they scheme together against me,
　　　　and plot to take my life.
14　But my trust is in you, O Lord. ◆
　　　I have said, 'You are my God.

15 'My times are in your hand; ♦
deliver me from the hand of my enemies,
and from those who persecute me.
16 'Make your face to shine upon your servant, ♦
and save me for your mercy's sake.'
17 Lord, let me not be confounded
for I have called upon you; ♦
but let the wicked be put to shame;
let them be silent in the grave.
18 Let the lying lips be put to silence ♦
that speak against the righteous
with arrogance, disdain and contempt.

19 How abundant is your goodness, O Lord,
which you have laid up for those who fear you; ♦
which you have prepared in the sight of all
for those who put their trust in you.
20 You hide them in the shelter of your presence
from those who slander them; ♦
you keep them safe in your refuge from the strife of tongues.
21 Blessed be the Lord! ♦
For he has shown me his steadfast love
when I was as a city besieged.
22 I had said in my alarm,
'I have been cut off from the sight of your eyes.' ♦
Nevertheless, you heard the voice of my prayer
when I cried out to you.
23 Love the Lord, all you his servants; ♦
for the Lord protects the faithful,
but repays to the full the proud.
24 Be strong and let your heart take courage, ♦
all you who wait in hope for the Lord.

Psalm 32

1 Happy the one whose transgression is forgiven, ♦
and whose sin is covered.
2 Happy the one to whom the Lord imputes no guilt, ♦
and in whose spirit there is no guile.

3   For I held my tongue; ◆
    my bones wasted away
        through my groaning all the day long.
4   Your hand was heavy upon me day and night; ◆
    my moisture was dried up like the drought in summer.
5   Then I acknowledged my sin to you ◆
    and my iniquity I did not hide.
6   I said, 'I will confess my transgressions to the Lord,' ◆
    and you forgave the guilt of my sin.
7   Therefore let all the faithful make their prayers to you
        in time of trouble; ◆
    in the great water flood, it shall not reach them.
8   You are a place for me to hide in;
        you preserve me from trouble; ◆
    you surround me with songs of deliverance.

9   'I will instruct you and teach you
        in the way that you should go; ◆
    I will guide you with my eye.
10 'Be not like horse and mule which have no understanding; ◆
    whose mouths must be held with bit and bridle,
        or else they will not stay near you.'
11 Great tribulations remain for the wicked, ◆
    but mercy embraces those who trust in the Lord.
12 Be glad, you righteous, and rejoice in the Lord; ◆
    shout for joy, all who are true of heart.

Psalm 33

1   Rejoice in the Lord, O you righteous, ◆
    for it is good for the just to sing praises.
2   Praise the Lord with the lyre; ◆
    on the ten-stringed harp sing his praise.
3   Sing for him a new song; ◆
    play skilfully, with shouts of praise.
4   For the word of the Lord is true ◆
    and all his works are sure.
5   He loves righteousness and justice; ◆
    the earth is full of the loving-kindness of the Lord.

6   By the word of the Lord were the heavens made ◆
    and all their host by the breath of his mouth.
7   He gathers up the waters of the sea as in a waterskin ◆
    and lays up the deep in his treasury.
8   Let all the earth fear the Lord; ◆
    stand in awe of him, all who dwell in the world.
9   For he spoke, and it was done; ◆
    he commanded, and it stood fast.
10 The Lord brings the counsel of the nations to naught; ◆
    he frustrates the designs of the peoples.
11 But the counsel of the Lord shall endure for ever ◆
    and the designs of his heart from generation to generation.
12 Happy the nation whose God is the Lord ◆
    and the people he has chosen for his own.
13 The Lord looks down from heaven ◆
    and beholds all the children of earth.
14 From where he sits enthroned he turns his gaze ◆
    on all who dwell on the earth.
15 He fashions all the hearts of them ◆
    and understands all their works.
16 No king is saved by the might of his host; ◆
    no warrior delivered by his great strength.
17 A horse is a vain hope for deliverance; ◆
    for all its strength it cannot save.

18 Behold, the eye of the Lord
        is upon those who fear him, ◆
    on those who wait in hope for his steadfast love,
19 To deliver their soul from death ◆
    and to feed them in time of famine.
20 Our soul waits longingly for the Lord; ◆
    he is our help and our shield.
21 Indeed, our heart rejoices in him; ◆
    in his holy name have we put our trust.
22 Let your loving-kindness, O Lord, be upon us, ◆
    as we have set our hope on you.

1   I will bless the Lord at all times; ◆
       his praise shall ever be in my mouth.

2   My soul shall glory in the Lord; ◆
       let the humble hear and be glad.

3   O magnify the Lord with me; ◆
       let us exalt his name together.

4   I sought the Lord and he answered me ◆
       and delivered me from all my fears.

5   Look upon him and be radiant ◆
       and your faces shall not be ashamed.

6   This poor soul cried, and the Lord heard me ◆
       and saved me from all my troubles.

7   The angel of the Lord encamps around those who fear him ◆
       and delivers them.

8   O taste and see that the Lord is gracious; ◆
       blessed is the one who trusts in him.

9   Fear the Lord, all you his holy ones, ◆
       for those who fear him lack nothing.

10   Lions may lack and suffer hunger, ◆
       but those who seek the Lord
         lack nothing that is good.

11   Come, my children, and listen to me; ◆
       I will teach you the fear of the Lord.

12   Who is there who delights in life ◆
       and longs for days to enjoy good things?

13   Keep your tongue from evil ◆
       and your lips from lying words.

14   Turn from evil and do good; ◆
       seek peace and pursue it.

15   The eyes of the Lord are upon the righteous ◆
       and his ears are open to their cry.

16   The face of the Lord is against those who do evil, ◆
       to root out the remembrance of them from the earth.

17   The righteous cry and the Lord hears them ◆
       and delivers them out of all their troubles.

18   The Lord is near to the brokenhearted ◆
       and will save those who are crushed in spirit.

19   Many are the troubles of the righteous; ◆
      from them all will the Lord deliver them.
20   He keeps all their bones, ◆
      so that not one of them is broken.
21   But evil shall slay the wicked ◆
      and those who hate the righteous will be condemned.
22   The Lord ransoms the life of his servants ◆
      and will condemn none who seek refuge in him.

Psalm 36

5   Your love, O Lord, reaches to the heavens ◆
      and your faithfulness to the clouds.
6   Your righteousness stands like the strong mountains,
          your justice like the great deep; ◆
      you, Lord, shall save both man and beast.
7   How precious is your loving mercy, O God! ◆
      All mortal flesh shall take refuge
          under the shadow of your wings.
8   They shall be satisfied with the abundance of your house; ◆
      they shall drink from the river of your delights.
9   For with you is the well of life ◆
      and in your light shall we see light.
10   O continue your loving-kindness to those who know you ◆
      and your righteousness to those who are true of heart.

Psalm 37

1   Fret not because of evildoers; ◆
      be not jealous of those who do wrong.
2   For they shall soon wither like grass ◆
      and like the green herb fade away.
3   Trust in the Lord and be doing good; ◆
      dwell in the land and be nourished with truth.
4   Let your delight be in the Lord ◆
      and he will give you your heart's desire.
5   Commit your way to the Lord and put your trust in him, ◆
      and he will bring it to pass.
6   He will make your righteousness as clear as the light ◆
      and your just dealing as the noonday.

7 Be still before the Lord and wait for him; ♦
do not fret over those that prosper
as they follow their evil schemes.

8 Refrain from anger and abandon wrath; ♦
do not fret, lest you be moved to do evil.

9 For evildoers shall be cut off, ♦
but those who wait upon the Lord shall possess the land.

10 Yet a little while and the wicked shall be no more; ♦
you will search for their place and find them gone.

11 But the lowly shall possess the land ♦
and shall delight in abundance of peace.

12 The wicked plot against the righteous ♦
and gnash at them with their teeth.

41 The Lord shall stand by them and deliver them; ♦
he shall deliver them from the wicked and shall save them,
because they have put their trust in him.

Psalm 40

1 I waited patiently for the Lord; ♦
he inclined to me and heard my cry.

2 He brought me out of the roaring pit,
out of the mire and clay; ♦
he set my feet upon a rock and made my footing sure.

3 He has put a new song in my mouth,
a song of praise to our God; ♦
many shall see and fear
and put their trust in the Lord.

4 Blessed is the one who trusts in the Lord, ♦
who does not turn to the proud that follow a lie.

5 Great are the wonders you have done, O Lord my God.
How great your designs for us! ♦
There is none that can be compared with you.

6 If I were to proclaim them and tell of them ♦
they would be more than I am able to express.

7 Sacrifice and offering you do not desire ♦
but my ears you have opened;

8   Burnt offering and sacrifice for sin you have not required; ♦
      then said I: 'Lo, I come.

9   'In the scroll of the book it is written of me
        that I should do your will, O my God; ♦
      I delight to do it: your law is within my heart.'

10   I have declared your righteousness in the great congregation; ♦
      behold, I did not restrain my lips,
        and that, O Lord, you know.

11   Your righteousness I have not hidden in my heart;
        I have spoken of your faithfulness and your salvation; ♦
      I have not concealed your loving-kindness and truth
        from the great congregation.

Psalm 41

1   Blessed are those who consider the poor and needy; ♦
      the Lord will deliver them in the time of trouble.

2   The Lord preserves them and restores their life,
        that they may be happy in the land; ♦
      he will not hand them over to the will of their enemies.

3   The Lord sustains them on their sickbed; ♦
      their sickness, Lord, you will remove.

4   And so I said, 'Lord, be merciful to me; ♦
      heal me, for I have sinned against you.'

5   My enemies speak evil about me, ♦
      asking when I shall die and my name perish.

6   If they come to see me, they utter empty words; ♦
      their heart gathers mischief;
        when they go out, they tell it abroad.

7   All my enemies whisper together against me, ♦
      against me they devise evil,

8   Saying that a deadly thing has laid hold on me, ♦
      and that I will not rise again from where I lie.

9   Even my bosom friend, whom I trusted,
        who ate of my bread, ♦
      has lifted up his heel against me.

10   But you, O Lord, be merciful to me ♦
      and raise me up, that I may reward them.

11   By this I know that you favour me, ♦
     that my enemy does not triumph over me.

12   Because of my integrity you uphold me ♦
     and will set me before your face for ever.

13   Blessed be the Lord God of Israel, ♦
     from everlasting to everlasting. Amen and Amen.

Psalm 42

1   As the deer longs for the water brooks, ♦
     so longs my soul for you, O God.

2   My soul is athirst for God, even for the living God; ♦
     when shall I come before the presence of God?

3   My tears have been my bread day and night, ♦
     while all day long they say to me, 'Where is now your God?'

4   Now when I think on these things, I pour out my soul: ♦
     how I went with the multitude
       and led the procession to the house of God,

5   With the voice of praise and thanksgiving, ♦
     among those who kept holy day.

6   *Why are you so full of heaviness, O my soul, ♦*
     and why are you so disquieted within me?

7   *O put your trust in God; ♦*
     for I will yet give him thanks,
       who is the help of my countenance, and my God.

8   My soul is heavy within me; ♦
     therefore I will remember you from the land of Jordan,
       and from Hermon and the hill of Mizar.

9   Deep calls to deep in the thunder of your waterfalls; ♦
     all your breakers and waves have gone over me.

10   The Lord will grant his loving-kindness in the daytime; ♦
     through the night his song will be with me,
       a prayer to the God of my life.

11   I say to God my rock,
     'Why have you forgotten me, ♦
    and why go I so heavily, while the enemy oppresses me?'

12   As they crush my bones, my enemies mock me; ♦
     while all day long they say to me, 'Where is now your God?'

13 *Why are you so full of heaviness, O my soul, ♦*
    and why are you so disquieted within me?

14 *O put your trust in God; ♦*
    for I will yet give him thanks,
        who is the help of my countenance, and my God.

Psalm 43

1 Give judgement for me, O God,
       and defend my cause against an ungodly people; ♦
   deliver me from the deceitful and the wicked.

2 For you are the God of my refuge;
       why have you cast me from you, ♦
   and why go I so heavily, while the enemy oppresses me?

3 O send out your light and your truth, that they may lead me, ♦
   and bring me to your holy hill and to your dwelling,

4 That I may go to the altar of God,
       to the God of my joy and gladness; ♦
   and on the lyre I will give thanks to you, O God my God.

5 *Why are you so full of heaviness, O my soul, ♦*
   and why are you so disquieted within me?

6 *O put your trust in God; ♦*
   for I will yet give him thanks,
       who is the help of my countenance, and my God.

Psalm 45

1 My heart is astir with gracious words; ♦
   as I make my song for the king,
       my tongue is the pen of a ready writer.

2 You are the fairest of men; ♦
   full of grace are your lips,
       for God has blest you for ever.

7 You love righteousness and hate iniquity; ♦
   therefore God, your God, has anointed you
       with the oil of gladness above your fellows.

8 All your garments are fragrant with myrrh, aloes and cassia; ♦
   from ivory palaces the music of strings makes you glad.

9 Kings' daughters are among your honourable women; ♦
   at your right hand stands the queen in gold of Ophir.

10   Hear, O daughter; consider and incline your ear; ◆
        forget your own people and your father's house.

11   So shall the king have pleasure in your beauty; ◆
        he is your lord, so do him honour.

12   The people of Tyre shall bring you gifts; ◆
        the richest of the people shall seek your favour.

13   The king's daughter is all glorious within; ◆
        her clothing is embroidered cloth of gold.

14   She shall be brought to the king in raiment of needlework; ◆
        after her the virgins that are her companions.

15   With joy and gladness shall they be brought ◆
        and enter into the palace of the king.

16   'Instead of your fathers you shall have sons, ◆
        whom you shall make princes over all the land.

17   'I will make your name to be remembered
           through all generations; ◆
        therefore shall the peoples praise you for ever and ever.'

Psalm 46

1   God is our refuge and strength, ◆
        a very present help in trouble;

2   Therefore we will not fear, though the earth be moved, ◆
        and though the mountains tremble in the heart of the sea;

3   Though the waters rage and swell, ◆
        and though the mountains quake at the towering seas.

4   There is a river whose streams make glad the city of God, ◆
        the holy place of the dwelling of the Most High.

5   God is in the midst of her;
           therefore shall she not be removed; ◆
        God shall help her at the break of day.

6   The nations are in uproar and the kingdoms are shaken, ◆
        but God utters his voice and the earth shall melt away.

7   *The Lord of hosts is with us;* ◆
        the God of Jacob is our stronghold.

8   Come and behold the works of the Lord, ◆
        what destruction he has wrought upon the earth.

9   He makes wars to cease in all the world; ◆
he shatters the bow and snaps the spear
    and burns the chariots in the fire.

10   'Be still, and know that I am God; ◆
I will be exalted among the nations;
    I will be exalted in the earth.'

11   *The Lord of hosts is with us;* ◆
the God of Jacob is our stronghold.

Psalm 47

1   Clap your hands together, all you peoples; ◆
O sing to God with shouts of joy.

2   For the Lord Most High is to be feared; ◆
he is the great King over all the earth.

3   He subdued the peoples under us ◆
and the nations under our feet.

4   He has chosen our heritage for us, ◆
the pride of Jacob, whom he loves.

5   God has gone up with a merry noise, ◆
the Lord with the sound of the trumpet.

6   O sing praises to God, sing praises; ◆
sing praises to our King, sing praises.

7   For God is the King of all the earth; ◆
sing praises with all your skill.

8   God reigns over the nations; ◆
God has taken his seat upon his holy throne.

9   The nobles of the peoples are gathered together ◆
with the people of the God of Abraham.

10   For the powers of the earth belong to God ◆
and he is very highly exalted.

Psalm 48

1   Great is the Lord and highly to be praised, ◆
in the city of our God.

2   His holy mountain is fair and lifted high, ◆
the joy of all the earth.

3   On Mount Zion, the divine dwelling place, ◆
stands the city of the great king.

4   In her palaces God has shown himself ◆
     to be a sure refuge.

5   For behold, the kings of the earth assembled ◆
     and swept forward together.
6   They saw, and were dumbfounded; ◆
     dismayed, they fled in terror.
7   Trembling seized them there;
         they writhed like a woman in labour, ◆
     as when the east wind shatters the ships of Tarshish.
8   As we had heard, so have we seen
         in the city of the Lord of hosts, the city of our God: ◆
     God has established her for ever.

9   We have waited on your loving-kindness, O God, ◆
     in the midst of your temple.
10   As with your name, O God,
         so your praise reaches to the ends of the earth; ◆
     your right hand is full of justice.
11   Let Mount Zion rejoice and the daughters of Judah be glad, ◆
     because of your judgements, O Lord.
12   Walk about Zion and go round about her;
         count all her towers; ◆
     consider well her bulwarks; pass through her citadels,
13   That you may tell those who come after
         that such is our God for ever and ever. ◆
     It is he that shall be our guide for evermore.

Psalm 49

1   Hear this, all you peoples; ◆
     listen, all you that dwell in the world,
2   You of low or high degree, ◆
     both rich and poor together.
3   My mouth shall speak of wisdom ◆
     and my heart shall meditate on understanding.
4   I will incline my ear to a parable; ◆
     I will unfold my riddle with the lyre.

5 Why should I fear in evil days, ♦
   when the malice of my foes surrounds me,
6 Such as trust in their goods ♦
   and glory in the abundance of their riches?
7 For no one can indeed ransom another ♦
   or pay to God the price of deliverance.
8 To ransom a soul is too costly; ♦
   there is no price one could pay for it,
9 So that they might live for ever, ♦
   and never see the grave.
10 For we see that the wise die also;
     with the foolish and ignorant they perish ♦
   and leave their riches to others.
11 Their tomb is their home for ever,
     their dwelling through all generations, ♦
   though they call their lands after their own names.
12 Those who have honour, but lack understanding, ♦
   are like the beasts that perish.

Psalm 50

1 The Lord, the most mighty God, has spoken ♦
   and called the world from the rising of the sun to its setting.
2 Out of Zion, perfect in beauty, God shines forth; ♦
   our God comes and will not keep silence.
3 Consuming fire goes out before him ♦
   and a mighty tempest stirs about him.
4 He calls the heaven above, ♦
   and the earth, that he may judge his people:
5 'Gather to me my faithful, ♦
   who have sealed my covenant with sacrifice.'
6 Let the heavens declare his righteousness, ♦
   for God himself is judge.

7 Hear, O my people, and I will speak: ♦
   'I will testify against you, O Israel;
     for I am God, your God.
8 'I will not reprove you for your sacrifices, ♦
   for your burnt offerings are always before me.

9   'I will take no bull out of your house, ◆
     nor he-goat out of your folds,

10   'For all the beasts of the forest are mine, ◆
     the cattle upon a thousand hills.

11   'I know every bird of the mountains ◆
     and the insect of the field is mine.

12   'If I were hungry, I would not tell you, ◆
     for the whole world is mine and all that fills it.

13   'Do you think I eat the flesh of bulls, ◆
     or drink the blood of goats?

14   'Offer to God a sacrifice of thanksgiving ◆
     and fulfil your vows to God Most High.

15   'Call upon me in the day of trouble; ◆
     I will deliver you and you shall honour me.'

Psalm 51

1   Have mercy on me, O God, in your great goodness; ◆
     according to the abundance of your compassion
          blot out my offences.

2   Wash me thoroughly from my wickedness ◆
     and cleanse me from my sin.

3   For I acknowledge my faults ◆
     and my sin is ever before me.

4   Against you only have I sinned ◆
     and done what is evil in your sight,

5   So that you are justified in your sentence ◆
     and righteous in your judgement.

6   I have been wicked even from my birth, ◆
     a sinner when my mother conceived me.

7   Behold, you desire truth deep within me ◆
     and shall make me understand wisdom
          in the depths of my heart.

8   Purge me with hyssop and I shall be clean; ◆
     wash me and I shall be whiter than snow.

9   Make me hear of joy and gladness, ◆
     that the bones you have broken may rejoice.

10   Turn your face from my sins ◆
     and blot out all my misdeeds.

11   Make me a clean heart, O God, ◆
     and renew a right spirit within me.

12 Cast me not away from your presence ◆
   and take not your holy spirit from me.
13 Give me again the joy of your salvation ◆
   and sustain me with your gracious spirit;
14 Then shall I teach your ways to the wicked ◆
   and sinners shall return to you.
15 Deliver me from my guilt, O God,
      the God of my salvation, ◆
   and my tongue shall sing of your righteousness.
16 O Lord, open my lips ◆
   and my mouth shall proclaim your praise.
17 For you desire no sacrifice, else I would give it; ◆
   you take no delight in burnt offerings.
18 The sacrifice of God is a broken spirit; ◆
   a broken and contrite heart, O God, you will not despise.

Psalm 52

1 Why do you glory in evil, you tyrant, ◆
   while the goodness of God endures continually?
2 You plot destruction, you deceiver; ◆
   your tongue is like a sharpened razor.
3 You love evil rather than good, ◆
   falsehood rather than the word of truth.
4 You love all words that hurt, ◆
   O you deceitful tongue.
5 Therefore God shall utterly bring you down; ◆
   he shall take you and pluck you out of your tent
      and root you out of the land of the living.
6 The righteous shall see this and tremble; ◆
   they shall laugh you to scorn, and say:
7 'This is the one who did not take God for a refuge, ◆
   but trusted in great riches and relied upon wickedness.'

8 But I am like a spreading olive tree in the house of God; ◆
   I trust in the goodness of God for ever and ever.
9 I will always give thanks to you for what you have done; ◆
   I will hope in your name,
      for your faithful ones delight in it.

Psalm 54

1   Save me, O God, by your name ◆
    and vindicate me by your power.

2   Hear my prayer, O God; ◆
    give heed to the words of my mouth.

3   For strangers have risen up against me,
        and the ruthless seek after my life; ◆
    they have not set God before them.

4   Behold, God is my helper; ◆
    it is the Lord who upholds my life.

5   May evil rebound on those who lie in wait for me; ◆
    destroy them in your faithfulness.

6   An offering of a free heart will I give you ◆
    and praise your name, O Lord, for it is gracious.

7   For he has delivered me out of all my trouble, ◆
    and my eye has seen the downfall of my enemies.

Psalm 62

6   He alone is my rock and my salvation, ◆
    my stronghold, so that I shall not be shaken.

7   In God is my strength and my glory; ◆
    God is my strong rock; in him is my refuge.

8   Put your trust in him always, my people; ◆
    pour out your hearts before him, for God is our refuge.

9   The peoples are but a breath,
        the whole human race a deceit; ◆
    on the scales they are altogether lighter than air.

10 Put no trust in oppression; in robbery take no empty pride; ◆
    though wealth increase, set not your heart upon it.

11 God spoke once, and twice have I heard the same, ◆
    that power belongs to God.

12 Steadfast love belongs to you, O Lord, ◆
    for you repay everyone according to their deeds.

Psalm 63

1   O God, you are my God; eagerly I seek you; ◆
    my soul is athirst for you.

2   My flesh also faints for you, ◆
    as in a dry and thirsty land where there is no water.

3   So would I gaze upon you in your holy place, ◆
    that I might behold your power and your glory.
4   Your loving-kindness is better than life itself ◆
    and so my lips shall praise you.
5   I will bless you as long as I live ◆
    and lift up my hands in your name.
6   My soul shall be satisfied, as with marrow and fatness, ◆
    and my mouth shall praise you with joyful lips,
7   When I remember you upon my bed ◆
    and meditate on you in the watches of the night.
8   For you have been my helper ◆
    and under the shadow of your wings will I rejoice.

Psalm 65

1   Praise is due to you, O God, in Zion; ◆
    to you that answer prayer shall vows be paid.
2   To you shall all flesh come to confess their sins; ◆
    when our misdeeds prevail against us,
        you will purge them away.
3   Happy are they whom you choose
        and draw to your courts to dwell there. ◆
    We shall be satisfied with the blessings of your house,
        even of your holy temple.
4   With wonders you will answer us in your righteousness,
        O God of our salvation, ◆
    O hope of all the ends of the earth
        and of the farthest seas.
5   In your strength you set fast the mountains ◆
    and are girded about with might.
6   You still the raging of the seas, ◆
    the roaring of their waves
        and the clamour of the peoples.
7   Those who dwell at the ends of the earth
        tremble at your marvels; ◆
    the gates of the morning and evening sing your praise.

8   You visit the earth and water it; ◆
    you make it very plenteous.

9   The river of God is full of water; ◆
you prepare grain for your people,
    for so you provide for the earth.

10   You drench the furrows and smooth out the ridges; ◆
you soften the ground with showers and bless its increase.

11   You crown the year with your goodness, ◆
and your paths overflow with plenty.

12   May the pastures of the wilderness flow with goodness ◆
and the hills be girded with joy.

13   May the meadows be clothed with flocks of sheep ◆
and the valleys stand so thick with corn
    that they shall laugh and sing.

Psalm 66

1   Be joyful in God, all the earth; ◆
sing the glory of his name;
    sing the glory of his praise.

2   Say to God, 'How awesome are your deeds! ◆
Because of your great strength
    your enemies shall bow before you.

3   'All the earth shall worship you, ◆
sing to you, sing praise to your name.'

4   Come now and behold the works of God, ◆
how wonderful he is in his dealings with humankind.

5   He turned the sea into dry land;
    the river they passed through on foot; ◆
there we rejoiced in him.

6   In his might he rules for ever;
    his eyes keep watch over the nations; ◆
let no rebel rise up against him.

7   Bless our God, O you peoples; ◆
make the voice of his praise to be heard,

8   Who holds our souls in life ◆
and suffers not our feet to slip.

9   For you, O God, have proved us; ◆
you have tried us as silver is tried.

10   You brought us into the snare; ♦
     you laid heavy burdens upon our backs.
11   You let enemies ride over our heads;
         we went through fire and water; ♦
     but you brought us out into a place of liberty.

12   I will come into your house with burnt offerings
         and will pay you my vows, ♦
     which my lips uttered
         and my mouth promised when I was in trouble.
13   I will offer you fat burnt sacrifices
         with the smoke of rams; ♦
     I will sacrifice oxen and goats.

14   Come and listen, all you who fear God, ♦
     and I will tell you what he has done for my soul.
15   I called out to him with my mouth ♦
     and his praise was on my tongue.
16   If I had nursed evil in my heart, ♦
     the Lord would not have heard me,
17   But in truth God has heard me; ♦
     he has heeded the voice of my prayer.
18   Blessed be God, who has not rejected my prayer, ♦
     nor withheld his loving mercy from me.

Psalm 67

1   God be gracious to us and bless us ♦
     and make his face to shine upon us,
2   That your way may be known upon earth, ♦
     your saving power among all nations.
3   *Let the peoples praise you, O God;* ♦
     let all the peoples praise you.
4   O let the nations rejoice and be glad, ♦
     for you will judge the peoples righteously
         and govern the nations upon earth.
5   *Let the peoples praise you, O God;* ♦
     let all the peoples praise you.
6   Then shall the earth bring forth her increase, ♦
     and God, our own God, will bless us.

7   God will bless us, ♦
     and all the ends of the earth shall fear him.

Psalm 68

1   Let God arise and let his enemies be scattered; ♦
     let those that hate him flee before him.
2   As the smoke vanishes, so may they vanish away; ♦
     as wax melts at the fire,
          so let the wicked perish at the presence of God.
3   But let the righteous be glad and rejoice before God; ♦
     let them make merry with gladness.
4   Sing to God, sing praises to his name;
          exalt him who rides on the clouds. ♦
     The Lord is his name; rejoice before him.
5   Father of the fatherless, defender of widows, ♦
     God in his holy habitation!
6   God gives the solitary a home
          and brings forth prisoners to songs of welcome, ♦
     but the rebellious inhabit a burning desert.

7   O God, when you went forth before your people, ♦
     when you marched through the wilderness,
8   The earth shook and the heavens dropped down rain,
          at the presence of God, the Lord of Sinai, ♦
     at the presence of God, the God of Israel.
9   You sent down a gracious rain, O God; ♦
     you refreshed your inheritance when it was weary.
10   Your people came to dwell there; ♦
     in your goodness, O God, you provide for the poor.

33   He rides on the ancient heaven of heavens ♦
     and sends forth his voice, a mighty voice.
34   Ascribe power to God, whose splendour is over Israel, ♦
     whose power is above the clouds.
35   How terrible is God in his holy sanctuary, ♦
     the God of Israel, who gives power and strength to his people!
          Blessed be God.

8   For your sake have I suffered reproach; ◆
shame has covered my face.

9   I have become a stranger to my kindred, ◆
an alien to my mother's children.

10   Zeal for your house has eaten me up; ◆
the scorn of those who scorn you has fallen upon me.

11   I humbled myself with fasting, ◆
but that was turned to my reproach.

12   I put on sackcloth also ◆
and became a byword among them.

13   Those who sit at the gate murmur against me, ◆
and the drunkards make songs about me.

14   But as for me, I make my prayer to you, O Lord; ◆
at an acceptable time, O God.

15   Answer me, O God, in the abundance of your mercy ◆
and with your sure salvation.

16   Draw me out of the mire, that I sink not; ◆
let me be rescued from those who hate me
and out of the deep waters.

17   Let not the water flood drown me,
neither the deep swallow me up; ◆
let not the Pit shut its mouth upon me.

18   Answer me, Lord, for your loving-kindness is good; ◆
turn to me in the multitude of your mercies.

19   Hide not your face from your servant; ◆
be swift to answer me, for I am in trouble.

20   Draw near to my soul and redeem me; ◆
deliver me because of my enemies.

1   O God, make speed to save me; ◆
O Lord, make haste to help me.

2   Let those who seek my life
be put to shame and confusion; ◆
let them be turned back and disgraced
who wish me evil.

3　Let those who mock and deride me ◆
　　turn back because of their shame.
4　But let all who seek you rejoice and be glad in you; ◆
　　let those who love your salvation say always, 'Great is the Lord!'
5　As for me, I am poor and needy; ◆
　　come to me quickly, O God.
6　You are my help and my deliverer; ◆
　　O Lord, do not delay.

Psalm 71

1　In you, O Lord, do I seek refuge; ◆
　　let me never be put to shame.
2　In your righteousness, deliver me and set me free; ◆
　　incline your ear to me and save me.
3　Be for me a stronghold to which I may ever resort; ◆
　　send out to save me, for you are my rock and my fortress.
4　Deliver me, my God, from the hand of the wicked, ◆
　　from the grasp of the evildoer and the oppressor.
5　For you are my hope, O Lord God, ◆
　　my confidence, even from my youth.
6　Upon you have I leaned from my birth,
　　　when you drew me from my mother's womb; ◆
　　my praise shall be always of you.

Psalm 72

1　Give the king your judgements, O God, ◆
　　and your righteousness to the son of a king.
2　Then shall he judge your people righteously ◆
　　and your poor with justice.
3　May the mountains bring forth peace, ◆
　　and the little hills righteousness for the people.
4　May he defend the poor among the people, ◆
　　deliver the children of the needy and crush the oppressor.
5　May he live as long as the sun and moon endure, ◆
　　from one generation to another.
6　May he come down like rain upon the mown grass, ◆
　　like the showers that water the earth.
7　In his time shall righteousness flourish, ◆
　　and abundance of peace
　　　till the moon shall be no more.

10   The kings of Tarshish and of the isles shall pay tribute; ♦
      the kings of Sheba and Seba shall bring gifts.
11   All kings shall fall down before him; ♦
      all nations shall do him service.
12   For he shall deliver the poor that cry out, ♦
      the needy and those who have no helper.
13   He shall have pity on the weak and poor; ♦
      he shall preserve the lives of the needy.
14   He shall redeem their lives from oppression and violence, ♦
      and dear shall their blood be in his sight.
15   Long may he live;
        unto him may be given gold from Sheba; ♦
      may prayer be made for him continually
        and may they bless him all the day long.
16   May there be abundance of grain on the earth,
        standing thick upon the hilltops; ♦
      may its fruit flourish like Lebanon
        and its grain grow like the grass of the field.
17   May his name remain for ever
        and be established as long as the sun endures; ♦
      may all nations be blest in him
        and call him blessed.

18   Blessed be the Lord, the God of Israel, ♦
      who alone does wonderful things.
19   And blessed be his glorious name for ever. ♦
      May all the earth be filled with his glory.
        Amen. Amen.

                                                          Psalm 77

 1   I cry aloud to God; ♦
      I cry aloud to God and he will hear me.
 2   In the day of my trouble I have sought the Lord; ♦
      by night my hand is stretched out and does not tire;
        my soul refuses comfort.

11   I will remember the works of the Lord ♦
      and call to mind your wonders of old time.

12   I will meditate on all your works ◆
       and ponder your mighty deeds.

13   Your way, O God, is holy; ◆
       who is so great a god as our God?

14   You are the God who worked wonders ◆
       and declared your power among the peoples.

15   With a mighty arm you redeemed your people, ◆
       the children of Jacob and Joseph.

16   The waters saw you, O God;
         the waters saw you and were afraid; ◆
       the depths also were troubled.

17   The clouds poured out water; the skies thundered; ◆
       your arrows flashed on every side;

18   The voice of your thunder was in the whirlwind;
         your lightnings lit up the ground; ◆
       the earth trembled and shook.

19   Your way was in the sea, and your paths in the great waters, ◆
       but your footsteps were not known.

20   You led your people like sheep ◆
       by the hand of Moses and Aaron.

Psalm 78

1   Hear my teaching, O my people; ◆
       incline your ears to the words of my mouth.

2   I will open my mouth in a parable; ◆
       I will pour forth mysteries from of old,

3   Such as we have heard and known, ◆
       which our forebears have told us.

4   We will not hide from their children,
         but will recount to generations to come, ◆
       the praises of the Lord and his power
         and the wonderful works he has done.

5   He laid a solemn charge on Jacob
         and made it a law in Israel, ◆
       which he commanded them to teach their children,

6   That the generations to come might know,
         and the children yet unborn, ◆
       that they in turn might tell it to their children;

7	So that they might put their trust in God ♦
	and not forget the deeds of God,
	but keep his commandments.

12	For he did marvellous things in the sight of their forebears, ♦
	in the land of Egypt, in the field of Zoan.
13	He divided the sea and let them pass through; ♦
	he made the waters stand still in a heap.
14	He led them with a cloud by day ♦
	and all the night through with a blaze of fire.
15	He split the hard rocks in the wilderness ♦
	and gave them drink as from the great deep.
16	He brought streams out of the rock ♦
	and made water gush out like rivers.

23	So he commanded the clouds above ♦
	and opened the doors of heaven.
24	He rained down upon them manna to eat ♦
	and gave them the grain of heaven.
25	So mortals ate the bread of angels; ♦
	he sent them food in plenty.
26	He caused the east wind to blow in the heavens ♦
	and led out the south wind by his might.
27	He rained flesh upon them as thick as dust ♦
	and winged fowl like the sand of the sea.
28	He let it fall in the midst of their camp ♦
	and round about their tents.
29	So they ate and were well filled, ♦
	for he gave them what they desired.

Psalm 79

1 O God, the heathen have come into your heritage; ♦
   your holy temple have they defiled
      and made Jerusalem a heap of stones.
2 The dead bodies of your servants they have given
      to be food for the birds of the air, ♦
   and the flesh of your faithful to the beasts of the field.
3 Their blood have they shed like water
      on every side of Jerusalem, ♦
   and there was no one to bury them.

4   We have become the taunt of our neighbours, ◆
the scorn and derision of those that are round about us.

5   Lord, how long will you be angry, for ever? ◆
How long will your jealous fury blaze like fire?

6   Pour out your wrath upon the nations that have not known you, ◆
and upon the kingdoms that have not called upon your name.

7   For they have devoured Jacob ◆
and laid waste his dwelling place.

8   Remember not against us our former sins; ◆
let your compassion make haste to meet us,
     for we are brought very low.

9   Help us, O God of our salvation, for the glory of your name; ◆
deliver us, and wipe away our sins for your name's sake.

Psalm 80

1   Hear, O Shepherd of Israel, ◆
you that led Joseph like a flock;

2   Shine forth, you that are enthroned upon the cherubim, ◆
before Ephraim, Benjamin and Manasseh.

3   Stir up your mighty strength ◆
and come to our salvation.

4   *Turn us again, O God;* ◆
show the light of your countenance, and we shall be saved.

5   O Lord God of hosts, ◆
how long will you be angry at your people's prayer?

6   You feed them with the bread of tears; ◆
you give them abundance of tears to drink.

7   You have made us the derision of our neighbours, ◆
and our enemies laugh us to scorn.

8   *Turn us again, O God of hosts;* ◆
show the light of your countenance, and we shall be saved.

9   You brought a vine out of Egypt; ◆
you drove out the nations and planted it.

10   You made room around it, ◆
and when it had taken root, it filled the land.

11   The hills were covered with its shadow ♦
       and the cedars of God by its boughs.
12   It stretched out its branches to the Sea ♦
       and its tendrils to the River.
13   Why then have you broken down its wall, ♦
       so that all who pass by pluck off its grapes?
14   The wild boar out of the wood tears it off, ♦
       and all the insects of the field devour it.

15   Turn again, O God of hosts, ♦
       look down from heaven and behold;
16   Cherish this vine which your right hand has planted, ♦
       and the branch that you made so strong for yourself.
17   Let those who burnt it with fire, who cut it down, ♦
       perish at the rebuke of your countenance.
18   Let your hand be upon the man at your right hand, ♦
       the son of man you made so strong for yourself.

Psalm 81

1   Sing merrily to God our strength, ♦
       shout for joy to the God of Jacob.
2   Take up the song and sound the timbrel, ♦
       the tuneful lyre with the harp.
3   Blow the trumpet at the new moon, ♦
       as at the full moon, upon our solemn feast day.
4   For this is a statute for Israel, ♦
       a law of the God of Jacob,
5   The charge he laid on the people of Joseph, ♦
       when they came out of the land of Egypt.
6   I heard a voice I did not know, that said: ♦
       'I eased their shoulder from the burden;
         their hands were set free from bearing the load.
7   'You called upon me in trouble and I delivered you; ♦
       I answered you from the secret place of thunder
         and proved you at the waters of Meribah.
8   'Hear, O my people, and I will admonish you: ♦
       O Israel, if you would but listen to me!
9   'There shall be no strange god among you; ♦
       you shall not worship a foreign god.

10   'I am the Lord your God,
          who brought you up from the land of Egypt; ◆
      open your mouth wide and I shall fill it.'

11   But my people would not hear my voice ◆
      and Israel would not obey me.
12   So I sent them away in the stubbornness of their hearts, ◆
      and let them walk after their own counsels.
13   O that my people would listen to me, ◆
      that Israel would walk in my ways!
14   Then I should soon put down their enemies ◆
      and turn my hand against their adversaries.
15   Those who hate the Lord would be humbled before him, ◆
      and their punishment would last for ever.
16   But Israel would I feed with the finest wheat ◆
      and with honey from the rock would I satisfy them.

Psalm 82

1   God has taken his stand in the council of heaven; ◆
     in the midst of the gods he gives judgement:
2   'How long will you judge unjustly ◆
     and show such favour to the wicked?
3   'You were to judge the weak and the orphan; ◆
     defend the right of the humble and needy;
4   'Rescue the weak and the poor; ◆
     deliver them from the hand of the wicked.
5   'They have no knowledge or wisdom;
        they walk on still in darkness: ◆
     all the foundations of the earth are shaken.
6   'Therefore I say that though you are gods ◆
     and all of you children of the Most High,
7   'Nevertheless, you shall die like mortals ◆
     and fall like one of their princes.'
8   Arise, O God and judge the earth, ◆
     for it is you that shall take all nations for your possession.

Psalm 84

1   How lovely is your dwelling place, O Lord of hosts! ◆
     My soul has a desire and longing to enter the courts of the Lord;
        my heart and my flesh rejoice in the living God.

2 The sparrow has found her a house
    and the swallow a nest where she may lay her young: ♦
  at your altars, O Lord of hosts, my King and my God.

3 Blessed are they who dwell in your house: ♦
  they will always be praising you.

4 Blessed are those whose strength is in you, ♦
  in whose heart are the highways to Zion,

5 Who going through the barren valley find there a spring, ♦
  and the early rains will clothe it with blessing.

6 They will go from strength to strength ♦
  and appear before God in Zion.

7 O Lord God of hosts, hear my prayer; ♦
  listen, O God of Jacob.

8 Behold our defender, O God, ♦
  and look upon the face of your anointed.

9 For one day in your courts ♦
  is better than a thousand.

10 I would rather be a doorkeeper in the house of my God ♦
  than dwell in the tents of ungodliness.

11 For the Lord God is both sun and shield;
    he will give grace and glory; ♦
  no good thing shall the Lord withhold
    from those who walk with integrity.

12 O Lord God of hosts, ♦
  blessed are those who put their trust in you.

Psalm 85

1 Lord, you were gracious to your land; ♦
  you restored the fortunes of Jacob.

2 You forgave the offence of your people ♦
  and covered all their sins.

3 You laid aside all your fury ♦
  and turned from your wrathful indignation.

4 Restore us again, O God our Saviour, ♦
  and let your anger cease from us.

5 Will you be displeased with us for ever? ♦
  Will you stretch out your wrath from one generation to
      another?

6   Will you not give us life again, ◆
       that your people may rejoice in you?
7   Show us your mercy, O Lord, ◆
       and grant us your salvation.

8   I will listen to what the Lord God will say, ◆
       for he shall speak peace to his people and to the faithful,
          that they turn not again to folly.
9   Truly, his salvation is near to those who fear him, ◆
       that his glory may dwell in our land.
10   Mercy and truth are met together, ◆
       righteousness and peace have kissed each other;
11   Truth shall spring up from the earth ◆
       and righteousness look down from heaven.
12   The Lord will indeed give all that is good, ◆
       and our land will yield its increase.
13   Righteousness shall go before him ◆
       and direct his steps in the way.

Psalm 86

1   Incline your ear, O Lord, and answer me, ◆
       for I am poor and in misery.
2   Preserve my soul, for I am faithful; ◆
       save your servant, for I put my trust in you.
3   Be merciful to me, O Lord, for you are my God; ◆
       I call upon you all the day long.
4   Gladden the soul of your servant, ◆
       for to you, O Lord, I lift up my soul.
5   For you, Lord, are good and forgiving, ◆
       abounding in steadfast love to all who call upon you.
6   Give ear, O Lord, to my prayer ◆
       and listen to the voice of my supplication.
7   In the day of my distress I will call upon you, ◆
       for you will answer me.

8   Among the gods there is none like you, O Lord, ◆
       nor any works like yours.

9   All nations you have made shall come
        and worship you, O Lord, ◆
     and shall glorify your name.

10   For you are great and do wonderful things; ◆
     you alone are God.

11   Teach me your way, O Lord, and I will walk in your truth; ◆
     knit my heart to you, that I may fear your name.

12   I will thank you, O Lord my God, with all my heart, ◆
     and glorify your name for evermore;

13   For great is your steadfast love towards me, ◆
     for you have delivered my soul from the depths of the grave.

14   O God, the proud rise up against me
        and a ruthless horde seek after my life; ◆
     they have not set you before their eyes.

15   But you, Lord, are gracious and full of compassion, ◆
     slow to anger and full of kindness and truth.

16   Turn to me and have mercy upon me; ◆
     give your strength to your servant
        and save the child of your handmaid.

17   Show me a token of your favour,
        that those who hate me may see it and be ashamed; ◆
     because you, O Lord, have helped and comforted me.

Psalm 89

1   My song shall be always of the loving-kindness of the Lord: ◆
     with my mouth will I proclaim your faithfulness
        throughout all generations.

2   I will declare that your love is established for ever; ◆
     you have set your faithfulness as firm as the heavens.

3   For you said: 'I have made a covenant with my chosen one; ◆
     I have sworn an oath to David my servant:

4   ' "Your seed will I establish for ever ◆
     and build up your throne for all generations." '

15   Happy are the people who know the shout of triumph: ◆
     they walk, O Lord, in the light of your countenance.

16   In your name they rejoice all the day long ◆
     and are exalted in your righteousness.

17 For you are the glory of their strength, ♦
    and in your favour you lift up our heads.

18 Truly the Lord is our shield; ♦
    the Holy One of Israel is our king.

19 You spoke once in a vision and said to your faithful people: ♦
    'I have set a youth above the mighty;
        I have raised a young man over the people.

20 'I have found David my servant; ♦
    with my holy oil have I anointed him.

21 'My hand shall hold him fast ♦
    and my arm shall strengthen him.

22 'No enemy shall deceive him, ♦
    nor any wicked person afflict him.

23 'I will strike down his foes before his face ♦
    and beat down those that hate him.

24 'My truth also and my steadfast love shall be with him, ♦
    and in my name shall his head be exalted.

25 'I will set his dominion upon the sea ♦
    and his right hand upon the rivers.

26 'He shall call to me, "You are my Father, ♦
    my God, and the rock of my salvation;"

27 'And I will make him my firstborn, ♦
    the most high above the kings of the earth.

28 'The love I have pledged to him will I keep for ever, ♦
    and my covenant will stand fast with him.

29 'His seed also will I make to endure for ever ♦
    and his throne as the days of heaven.

30 'But if his children forsake my law ♦
    and cease to walk in my judgements,

31 'If they break my statutes ♦
    and do not keep my commandments,

32 'I will punish their offences with a rod ♦
    and their sin with scourges.

33 'But I will not take from him my steadfast love ♦
    nor suffer my truth to fail.

34 'My covenant will I not break ♦
    nor alter what has gone out of my lips.

35 'Once for all have I sworn by my holiness ♦
    that I will not prove false to David.

36 'His seed shall endure for ever ♦
   and his throne as the sun before me;
37 'It shall stand fast for ever as the moon, ♦
   the enduring witness in the heavens.'

Psalm 90

1 Lord, you have been our refuge ♦
   from one generation to another.
2 Before the mountains were brought forth,
     or the earth and the world were formed, ♦
   from everlasting to everlasting you are God.
3 You turn us back to dust and say: ♦
   'Turn back, O children of earth.'
4 For a thousand years in your sight are but as yesterday, ♦
   which passes like a watch in the night.
5 You sweep them away like a dream; ♦
   they fade away suddenly like the grass.
6 In the morning it is green and flourishes; ♦
   in the evening it is dried up and withered.
7 For we consume away in your displeasure; ♦
   we are afraid at your wrathful indignation.
8 You have set our misdeeds before you ♦
   and our secret sins in the light of your countenance.
9 When you are angry, all our days are gone; ♦
   our years come to an end like a sigh.
10 The days of our life are three score years and ten,
     or if our strength endures, even four score; ♦
   yet the sum of them is but labour and sorrow,
     for they soon pass away and we are gone.
11 Who regards the power of your wrath ♦
   and your indignation like those who fear you?
12 So teach us to number our days ♦
   that we may apply our hearts to wisdom.

13 Turn again, O Lord; how long will you delay? ♦
   Have compassion on your servants.
14 Satisfy us with your loving-kindness in the morning, ♦
   that we may rejoice and be glad all our days.
15 Give us gladness for the days you have afflicted us, ♦
   and for the years in which we have seen adversity.

16   Show your servants your works, ◆
and let your glory be over their children.

17   May the gracious favour of the Lord our God be upon us; ◆
prosper our handiwork; O prosper the work of our hands.

Psalm 91

1   Whoever dwells in the shelter of the Most High ◆
and abides under the shadow of the Almighty,

2   Shall say to the Lord, 'My refuge and my stronghold, ◆
my God, in whom I put my trust.'

3   For he shall deliver you from the snare of the fowler ◆
and from the deadly pestilence.

4   He shall cover you with his wings
      and you shall be safe under his feathers; ◆
his faithfulness shall be your shield and buckler.

5   You shall not be afraid of any terror by night, ◆
nor of the arrow that flies by day;

6   Of the pestilence that stalks in darkness, ◆
nor of the sickness that destroys at noonday.

9   Because you have made the Lord your refuge ◆
and the Most High your stronghold,

10   There shall no evil happen to you, ◆
neither shall any plague come near your tent.

11   For he shall give his angels charge over you, ◆
to keep you in all your ways.

12   They shall bear you in their hands, ◆
lest you dash your foot against a stone.

13   You shall tread upon the lion and adder; ◆
the young lion and the serpent you shall trample underfoot.

14   Because they have set their love upon me,
      therefore will I deliver them; ◆
I will lift them up, because they know my name.

15   They will call upon me and I will answer them; ◆
I am with them in trouble,
      I will deliver them and bring them to honour.

16   With long life will I satisfy them ◆
and show them my salvation.

1   It is a good thing to give thanks to the Lord ◆
    and to sing praises to your name, O Most High;
2   To tell of your love early in the morning ◆
    and of your faithfulness in the night-time,
3   Upon the ten-stringed instrument, upon the harp, ◆
    and to the melody of the lyre.
4   For you, Lord, have made me glad by your acts, ◆
    and I sing aloud at the works of your hands.

11 My eyes will look down on my foes; ◆
    my ears shall hear the ruin of the evildoers
        who rise up against me.
12 The righteous shall flourish like a palm tree, ◆
    and shall spread abroad like a cedar of Lebanon.
13 Such as are planted in the house of the Lord ◆
    shall flourish in the courts of our God.
14 They shall still bear fruit in old age; ◆
    they shall be vigorous and in full leaf;
15 That they may show that the Lord is true; ◆
    he is my rock,
        and there is no unrighteousness in him.

1   The Lord is king and has put on glorious apparel; ◆
    the Lord has put on his glory
        and girded himself with strength.
2   He has made the whole world so sure ◆
    that it cannot be moved.
3   Your throne has been established from of old; ◆
    you are from everlasting.
4   The floods have lifted up, O Lord,
        the floods have lifted up their voice; ◆
    the floods lift up their pounding waves.
5   Mightier than the thunder of many waters,
        mightier than the breakers of the sea, ◆
    the Lord on high is mightier.
6   Your testimonies are very sure; ◆
    holiness adorns your house, O Lord, for ever.

1   O come, let us sing to the Lord; ◆
let us heartily rejoice in the rock of our salvation.

2   Let us come into his presence with thanksgiving ◆
and be glad in him with psalms.

3   For the Lord is a great God ◆
and a great king above all gods.

4   In his hand are the depths of the earth ◆
and the heights of the mountains are his also.

5   The sea is his, for he made it, ◆
and his hands have moulded the dry land.

6   Come, let us worship and bow down ◆
and kneel before the Lord our Maker.

7   For he is our God; ◆
we are the people of his pasture and the sheep of his hand.

8   O that today you would listen to his voice: ◆
'Harden not your hearts as at Meribah,
on that day at Massah in the wilderness,

9   'When your forebears tested me, and put me to the proof, ◆
though they had seen my works.

10   'Forty years long I detested that generation and said, ◆
"This people are wayward in their hearts;
they do not know my ways."

11   'So I swore in my wrath, ◆
"They shall not enter into my rest." '

1   Sing to the Lord a new song; ◆
sing to the Lord, all the earth.

2   Sing to the Lord and bless his name; ◆
tell out his salvation from day to day.

3   Declare his glory among the nations ◆
and his wonders among all peoples.

4   For great is the Lord and greatly to be praised; ◆
he is more to be feared than all gods.

5   For all the gods of the nations are but idols; ◆
it is the Lord who made the heavens.

6   Honour and majesty are before him; ♦
    power and splendour are in his sanctuary.

7   Ascribe to the Lord, you families of the peoples; ♦
    ascribe to the Lord honour and strength.
8   Ascribe to the Lord the honour due to his name; ♦
    bring offerings and come into his courts.
9   O worship the Lord in the beauty of holiness; ♦
    let the whole earth tremble before him.
10 Tell it out among the nations that the Lord is king. ♦
    He has made the world so firm that it cannot be moved;
        he will judge the peoples with equity.

11 Let the heavens rejoice and let the earth be glad; ♦
    let the sea thunder and all that is in it;
12 Let the fields be joyful and all that is in them; ♦
    let all the trees of the wood shout for joy before the Lord.
13 For he comes, he comes to judge the earth; ♦
    with righteousness he will judge the world
        and the peoples with his truth.

Psalm 97

1   The Lord is king: let the earth rejoice; ♦
    let the multitude of the isles be glad.
2   Clouds and darkness are round about him; ♦
    righteousness and justice are the foundation of his throne.
3   Fire goes before him ♦
    and burns up his enemies on every side.

4   His lightnings lit up the world; ♦
    the earth saw it and trembled.
5   The mountains melted like wax at the presence of the Lord, ♦
    at the presence of the Lord of the whole earth.
6   The heavens declared his righteousness, ♦
    and all the peoples have seen his glory.

7   Confounded be all who worship carved images
        and delight in mere idols. ♦
    Bow down before him, all you gods.

8   Zion heard and was glad, and the daughters of Judah rejoiced, ♦
    because of your judgements, O Lord.
9   For you, Lord, are most high over all the earth; ♦
    you are exalted far above all gods.

10 The Lord loves those who hate evil; ♦
    he preserves the lives of his faithful
        and delivers them from the hand of the wicked.
11 Light has sprung up for the righteous ♦
    and joy for the true of heart.
12 Rejoice in the Lord, you righteous, ♦
    and give thanks to his holy name.

Psalm 98

1   Sing to the Lord a new song, ♦
    for he has done marvellous things.
2   His own right hand and his holy arm ♦
    have won for him the victory.
3   The Lord has made known his salvation; ♦
    his deliverance has he openly shown in the sight of the nations.
4   He has remembered his mercy and faithfulness
        towards the house of Israel, ♦
    and all the ends of the earth have seen the salvation of our God.

5   Sound praises to the Lord, all the earth; ♦
    break into singing and make music.
6   Make music to the Lord with the lyre, ♦
    with the lyre and the voice of melody.
7   With trumpets and the sound of the horn ♦
    sound praises before the Lord, the King.

8   Let the sea thunder and all that fills it, ♦
    the world and all that dwell upon it.
9   Let the rivers clap their hands ♦
    and let the hills ring out together before the Lord,
        for he comes to judge the earth.
10 In righteousness shall he judge the world ♦
    and the peoples with equity.

Psalm 99

1   The Lord is king: let the peoples tremble; ◆
    he is enthroned above the cherubim: let the earth shake.
2   The Lord is great in Zion ◆
    and high above all peoples.
3   Let them praise your name, which is great and awesome; ◆
    the Lord our God is holy.
4   Mighty king, who loves justice,
      you have established equity; ◆
    you have executed justice and righteousness in Jacob.
5   *Exalt the Lord our God;* ◆
    bow down before his footstool, for he is holy.

6   Moses and Aaron among his priests
      and Samuel among those who call upon his name; ◆
    they called upon the Lord and he answered them.
7   He spoke to them out of the pillar of cloud; ◆
    they kept his testimonies and the law that he gave them.
8   You answered them, O Lord our God; ◆
    you were a God who forgave them
    and pardoned them for their offences.
9   *Exalt the Lord our God*
      and worship him upon his holy hill, ◆
    for the Lord our God is holy.

Psalm 100

1   O be joyful in the Lord, all the earth; ◆
    serve the Lord with gladness
      and come before his presence with a song.
2   Know that the Lord is God; ◆
    it is he that has made us and we are his;
      we are his people and the sheep of his pasture.
3   Enter his gates with thanksgiving
      and his courts with praise; ◆
    give thanks to him and bless his name.
4   For the Lord is gracious; his steadfast love is everlasting, ◆
    and his faithfulness endures from generation to generation.

1   Bless the Lord, O my soul, ◆
    and all that is within me bless his holy name.

2   Bless the Lord, O my soul, ◆
    and forget not all his benefits;

3   Who forgives all your sins ◆
    and heals all your infirmities;

4   Who redeems your life from the Pit ◆
    and crowns you with faithful love and compassion;

5   Who satisfies you with good things, ◆
    so that your youth is renewed like an eagle's.

6   The Lord executes righteousness ◆
    and judgement for all who are oppressed.

7   He made his ways known to Moses ◆
    and his works to the children of Israel.

8   The Lord is full of compassion and mercy, ◆
    slow to anger and of great kindness.

9   He will not always accuse us, ◆
    neither will he keep his anger for ever.

10   He has not dealt with us according to our sins, ◆
    nor rewarded us according to our wickedness.

11   For as the heavens are high above the earth, ◆
    so great is his mercy upon those who fear him.

12   As far as the east is from the west, ◆
    so far has he set our sins from us.

13   As a father has compassion on his children, ◆
    so is the Lord merciful towards those who fear him.

19   The Lord has established his throne in heaven, ◆
    and his kingdom has dominion over all.

20   Bless the Lord, you angels of his, ◆
    you mighty ones who do his bidding
       and hearken to the voice of his word.

21   Bless the Lord, all you his hosts, ◆
    you ministers of his who do his will.

22   Bless the Lord, all you works of his,
       in all places of his dominion; ◆
    bless the Lord, O my soul.

1   Bless the Lord, O my soul. ✦
    O Lord my God, how excellent is your greatness!

2   You are clothed with majesty and honour, ✦
    wrapped in light as in a garment.

3   You spread out the heavens like a curtain ✦
    and lay the beams of your dwelling place in the waters above.

4   You make the clouds your chariot ✦
    and ride on the wings of the wind.

5   You make the winds your messengers ✦
    and flames of fire your servants.

6   You laid the foundations of the earth, ✦
    that it never should move at any time.

7   You covered it with the deep like a garment; ✦
    the waters stood high above the hills.

8   At your rebuke they fled; ✦
    at the voice of your thunder they hastened away.

9   They rose up to the hills and flowed down
        to the valleys beneath, ✦
    to the place which you had appointed for them.

25 People go forth to their work ✦
    and to their labour until the evening.

26 O Lord, how manifold are your works! ✦
    In wisdom you have made them all;
        the earth is full of your creatures.

27 There is the sea, spread far and wide, ✦
    and there move creatures beyond number, both small and great.

28 There go the ships, and there is that Leviathan ✦
    which you have made to play in the deep.

29 All of these look to you ✦
    to give them their food in due season.

30 When you give it them, they gather it; ✦
    you open your hand and they are filled with good.

31 When you hide your face they are troubled; ✦
    when you take away their breath,
        they die and return again to the dust.

32 When you send forth your spirit, they are created, ✦
    and you renew the face of the earth.

33 May the glory of the Lord endure for ever; ◆
    may the Lord rejoice in his works;
34 He looks on the earth and it trembles; ◆
    he touches the mountains and they smoke.
35 I will sing to the Lord as long as I live; ◆
    I will make music to my God while I have my being.
36 So shall my song please him ◆
    while I rejoice in the Lord.
37 Let sinners be consumed out of the earth
        and the wicked be no more. ◆
    Bless the Lord, O my soul.
        Alleluia.

Psalm 105

1   O give thanks to the Lord and call upon his name; ◆
    make known his deeds among the peoples.
2   Sing to him, sing praises, ◆
    and tell of all his marvellous works.
3   Rejoice in the praise of his holy name; ◆
    let the hearts of them rejoice who seek the Lord.
4   Seek the Lord and his strength; ◆
    seek his face continually.
5   Remember the marvels he has done, ◆
    his wonders and the judgements of his mouth,
6   O seed of Abraham his servant, ◆
    O children of Jacob his chosen.

16 Then he called down famine over the land ◆
    and broke every staff of bread.
17 But he had sent a man before them, ◆
    Joseph, who was sold as a slave.
18 They shackled his feet with fetters; ◆
    his neck was ringed with iron.
19 Until all he foretold came to pass, ◆
    the word of the Lord tested him.
20 The king sent and released him; ◆
    the ruler of peoples set him free.
21 He appointed him lord of his household ◆
    and ruler of all he possessed,

22   To instruct his princes as he willed ♦
        and to teach his counsellors wisdom.

23   Then Israel came into Egypt; ♦
        Jacob sojourned in the land of Ham.
24   And the Lord made his people exceedingly fruitful; ♦
        he made them too many for their adversaries,
25   Whose heart he turned, so that they hated his people ♦
        and dealt craftily with his servants.
26   Then sent he Moses his servant ♦
        and Aaron whom he had chosen.

37   Then he brought them out with silver and gold; ♦
        there was not one among their tribes that stumbled.
38   Egypt was glad at their departing, ♦
        for a dread of them had fallen upon them.
39   He spread out a cloud for a covering ♦
        and a fire to light up the night.
40   They asked and he brought them quails; ♦
        he satisfied them with the bread of heaven.
41   He opened the rock, and the waters gushed out ♦
        and ran in the dry places like a river.
42   For he remembered his holy word ♦
        and Abraham, his servant.
43   So he brought forth his people with joy, ♦
        his chosen ones with singing.
44   He gave them the lands of the nations ♦
        and they took possession of the fruit of their toil,
45   That they might keep his statutes ♦
        and faithfully observe his laws.
          Alleluia.

Psalm 106

1   Alleluia.
          Give thanks to the Lord, for he is gracious, ♦
        for his faithfulness endures for ever.
2   Who can express the mighty acts of the Lord ♦
        or show forth all his praise?

3   Blessed are those who observe what is right ◆
     and always do what is just.
4   Remember me, O Lord, in the favour you bear for your people; ◆
     visit me in the day of your salvation;
5   That I may see the prosperity of your chosen
       and rejoice in the gladness of your people, ◆
     and exult with your inheritance.

6   We have sinned like our forebears; ◆
     we have done wrong and dealt wickedly.

19   They made a calf at Horeb ◆
     and worshipped the molten image;
20   Thus they exchanged their glory ◆
     for the image of an ox that feeds on hay.
21   They forgot God their saviour, ◆
     who had done such great things in Egypt,
22   Wonderful deeds in the land of Ham ◆
     and fearful things at the Red Sea.
23   So he would have destroyed them,
       had not Moses his chosen stood before him in the breach, ◆
     to turn away his wrath from consuming them.

Psalm 107

1   O give thanks to the Lord, for he is gracious, ◆
     for his steadfast love endures for ever.
2   Let the redeemed of the Lord say this, ◆
     those he redeemed from the hand of the enemy,
3   And gathered out of the lands
       from the east and from the west, ◆
     from the north and from the south.

4   Some went astray in desert wastes ◆
     and found no path to a city to dwell in.
5   Hungry and thirsty, ◆
     their soul was fainting within them.
6   So they cried to the Lord in their trouble ◆
     and he delivered them from their distress.
7   He set their feet on the right way ◆
     till they came to a city to dwell in.

8   *Let them give thanks to the Lord for his goodness ♦*
        and the wonders he does for his children.

9   *For he satisfies the longing soul ♦*
        and fills the hungry soul with good.

17   Some were foolish and took a rebellious way, ♦
       and were plagued because of their wrongdoing.

18   Their soul abhorred all manner of food ♦
       and drew near to the gates of death.

19   Then they cried to the Lord in their trouble, ♦
       and he delivered them from their distress.

20   He sent forth his word and healed them, ♦
       and saved them from destruction.

21   *Let them give thanks to the Lord for his goodness ♦*
        and the wonders he does for his children.

22   *Let them offer him sacrifices of thanksgiving ♦*
        and tell of his acts with shouts of joy.

23   Those who go down to the sea in ships ♦
       and ply their trade in great waters,

24   These have seen the works of the Lord ♦
       and his wonders in the deep.

25   For at his word the stormy wind arose ♦
       and lifted up the waves of the sea.

26   They were carried up to the heavens
         and down again to the deep; ♦
       their soul melted away in their peril.

27   They reeled and staggered like a drunkard ♦
       and were at their wits' end.

28   Then they cried to the Lord in their trouble, ♦
       and he brought them out of their distress.

29   He made the storm be still ♦
       and the waves of the sea were calmed.

30   Then were they glad because they were at rest, ♦
       and he brought them to the haven they desired.

31   *Let them give thanks to the Lord for his goodness ♦*
        and the wonders he does for his children.

32   *Let them exalt him in the congregation of the people ♦*
        and praise him in the council of the elders.

33 The Lord turns rivers into wilderness ◆
and water springs into thirsty ground;

34 A fruitful land he makes a salty waste, ◆
because of the wickedness of those who dwell there.

35 He makes the wilderness a pool of water ◆
and water springs out of a thirsty land.

36 There he settles the hungry ◆
and they build a city to dwell in.

37 They sow fields and plant vineyards ◆
and bring in a fruitful harvest.

43 Whoever is wise will ponder these things ◆
and consider the loving-kindness of the Lord.

Psalm 111

1 Alleluia.
I will give thanks to the Lord with my whole heart, ◆
in the company of the faithful and in the congregation.

2 The works of the Lord are great, ◆
sought out by all who delight in them.

3 His work is full of majesty and honour ◆
and his righteousness endures for ever.

4 He appointed a memorial for his marvellous deeds; ◆
the Lord is gracious and full of compassion.

5 He gave food to those who feared him; ◆
he is ever mindful of his covenant.

6 He showed his people the power of his works ◆
in giving them the heritage of the nations.

7 The works of his hands are truth and justice; ◆
all his commandments are sure.

8 They stand fast for ever and ever; ◆
they are done in truth and equity.

9 He sent redemption to his people;
he commanded his covenant for ever; ◆
holy and awesome is his name.

10 The fear of the Lord is the beginning of wisdom;
a good understanding have those who live by it; ◆
his praise endures for ever.

1   Alleluia.
    Blessed are those who fear the Lord ◆
    and have great delight in his commandments.
2   Their descendants will be mighty in the land, ◆
    a generation of the faithful that will be blest.
3   Wealth and riches will be in their house, ◆
    and their righteousness endures for ever.
4   Light shines in the darkness for the upright; ◆
    gracious and full of compassion are the righteous.
5   It goes well with those who are generous in lending ◆
    and order their affairs with justice,
6   For they will never be shaken; ◆
    the righteous will be held in everlasting remembrance.
7   They will not be afraid of any evil tidings; ◆
    their heart is steadfast, trusting in the Lord.
8   Their heart is sustained and will not fear, ◆
    until they see the downfall of their foes.
9   They have given freely to the poor;
        their righteousness stands fast for ever; ◆
    their head will be exalted with honour.
10 The wicked shall see it and be angry;
        they shall gnash their teeth in despair; ◆
    the desire of the wicked shall perish.

1   Alleluia.
    Give praise, you servants of the Lord, ◆
    O praise the name of the Lord.
2   Blessed be the name of the Lord, ◆
    from this time forth and for evermore.
3   From the rising of the sun to its setting ◆
    let the name of the Lord be praised.
4   The Lord is high above all nations ◆
    and his glory above the heavens.
5   Who is like the Lord our God,
        that has his throne so high, ◆
    yet humbles himself to behold
        the things of heaven and earth?

6   He raises the poor from the dust ✦
    and lifts the needy from the ashes,

7   To set them with princes, ✦
    with the princes of his people.

8   He gives the barren woman a place in the house ✦
    and makes her a joyful mother of children.
       Alleluia.

Psalm 114

1   When Israel came out of Egypt, ✦
    the house of Jacob from a people of a strange tongue,

2   Judah became his sanctuary, ✦
    Israel his dominion.

3   The sea saw that, and fled; ✦
    Jordan was driven back.

4   The mountains skipped like rams, ✦
    the little hills like young sheep.

5   What ailed you, O sea, that you fled? ✦
    O Jordan, that you were driven back?

6   You mountains, that you skipped like rams, ✦
    you little hills like young sheep?

7   Tremble, O earth, at the presence of the Lord, ✦
    at the presence of the God of Jacob,

8   Who turns the hard rock into a pool of water, ✦
    the flint-stone into a springing well.

Psalm 116

1   I love the Lord,
       for he has heard the voice of my supplication; ✦
    because he inclined his ear to me
       on the day I called to him.

2   The snares of death encompassed me;
       the pains of hell took hold of me; ✦
    by grief and sorrow was I held.

3   Then I called upon the name of the Lord: ✦
    'O Lord, I beg you, deliver my soul.'

4   Gracious is the Lord and righteous; ✦
    our God is full of compassion.

5   The Lord watches over the simple; ✦
    I was brought very low and he saved me.

6   Turn again to your rest, O my soul, ◆
    for the Lord has been gracious to you.
7   For you have delivered my soul from death, ◆
    my eyes from tears and my feet from falling.
8   I will walk before the Lord ◆
    in the land of the living.

10 How shall I repay the Lord ◆
    for all the benefits he has given to me?
11 I will lift up the cup of salvation ◆
    and call upon the name of the Lord.
12 I will fulfil my vows to the Lord ◆
    in the presence of all his people.
13 Precious in the sight of the Lord ◆
    is the death of his faithful servants.
14 O Lord, I am your servant, ◆
    your servant, the child of your handmaid;
        you have freed me from my bonds.
15 I will offer to you a sacrifice of thanksgiving ◆
    and call upon the name of the Lord.
16 I will fulfil my vows to the Lord ◆
    in the presence of all his people,
17 In the courts of the house of the Lord, ◆
    in the midst of you, O Jerusalem.
        Alleluia.

Psalm 118

1   O give thanks to the Lord, for he is good; ◆
    his mercy endures for ever.
2   Let Israel now proclaim, ◆
    'His mercy endures for ever.'

14 The Lord is my strength and my song, ◆
    and he has become my salvation.
15 Joyful shouts of salvation ◆
    sound from the tents of the righteous:
16 'The right hand of the Lord does mighty deeds;
        the right hand of the Lord raises up; ◆
    the right hand of the Lord does mighty deeds.'

17   I shall not die, but live ◆
         and declare the works of the Lord.
18   The Lord has punished me sorely, ◆
         but he has not given me over to death.

19   Open to me the gates of righteousness, ◆
         that I may enter and give thanks to the Lord.
20   This is the gate of the Lord; ◆
         the righteous shall enter through it.
21   I will give thanks to you, for you have answered me ◆
         and have become my salvation.
22   The stone which the builders rejected ◆
         has become the chief cornerstone.
23   This is the Lord's doing, ◆
         and it is marvellous in our eyes.
24   This is the day that the Lord has made; ◆
         we will rejoice and be glad in it.
25   Come, O Lord, and save us we pray. ◆
         Come, Lord, send us now prosperity.
26   Blessed is he who comes in the name of the Lord; ◆
         we bless you from the house of the Lord.
27   The Lord is God; he has given us light; ◆
         link the pilgrims with cords
            right to the horns of the altar.

28   You are my God and I will thank you; ◆
         you are my God and I will exalt you.
29   O give thanks to the Lord, for he is good; ◆
         his mercy endures for ever.

Psalm 119

     1   Aleph
1   Blessed are those whose way is pure, ◆
         who walk in the law of the Lord.
2   Blessed are those who keep his testimonies ◆
         and seek him with their whole heart,
3   Those who do no wickedness, ◆
         but walk in his ways.

4   You, O Lord, have charged ♦
    that we should diligently keep your commandments.
5   O that my ways were made so direct ♦
    that I might keep your statutes.
6   Then should I not be put to shame, ♦
    because I have regard for all your commandments.
7   I will thank you with an unfeigned heart, ♦
    when I have learned your righteous judgements.
8   I will keep your statutes; ♦
    O forsake me not utterly.

    2   Beth
9   How shall young people cleanse their way ♦
    to keep themselves according to your word?
10 With my whole heart have I sought you; ♦
    O let me not go astray from your commandments.
11 Your words have I hidden within my heart, ♦
    that I should not sin against you.
12 Blessed are you, O Lord; ♦
    O teach me your statutes.
13 With my lips have I been telling ♦
    of all the judgements of your mouth.
14 I have taken greater delight in the way of your testimonies ♦
    than in all manner of riches.
15 I will meditate on your commandments ♦
    and contemplate your ways.
16 My delight shall be in your statutes ♦
    and I will not forget your word.

    5   He
33 Teach me, O Lord, the way of your statutes ♦
    and I shall keep it to the end.
34 Give me understanding and I shall keep your law; ♦
    I shall keep it with my whole heart.
35 Lead me in the path of your commandments, ♦
    for therein is my delight.
36 Incline my heart to your testimonies ♦
    and not to unjust gain.
37 Turn away my eyes lest they gaze on vanities; ♦
    O give me life in your ways.

38   Confirm to your servant your promise, ◆
      which stands for all who fear you.

39   Turn away the reproach which I dread, ◆
      because your judgements are good.

40   Behold, I long for your commandments; ◆
      in your righteousness give me life.

     13   Mem

97   Lord, how I love your law! ◆
      All the day long it is my study.

98   Your commandments have made me wiser than my enemies, ◆
      for they are ever with me.

99   I have more understanding than all my teachers, ◆
      for your testimonies are my meditation.

100   I am wiser than the aged, ◆
      because I keep your commandments.

101   I restrain my feet from every evil way, ◆
      that I may keep your word.

102   I have not turned aside from your judgements, ◆
      for you have been my teacher.

103   How sweet are your words on my tongue! ◆
      They are sweeter than honey to my mouth.

104   Through your commandments I get understanding; ◆
      therefore I hate all lying ways.

     14   Nun

105   Your word is a lantern to my feet ◆
      and a light upon my path.

106   I have sworn and will fulfil it, ◆
      to keep your righteous judgements.

107   I am troubled above measure; ◆
      give me life, O Lord, according to your word.

108   Accept the freewill offering of my mouth, O Lord, ◆
      and teach me your judgements.

109   My soul is ever in my hand, ◆
      yet I do not forget your law.

110   The wicked have laid a snare for me, ◆
      but I have not strayed from your commandments.

111 Your testimonies have I claimed as my heritage for ever; ◆
    for they are the very joy of my heart.
112 I have applied my heart to fulfil your statutes: ◆
    always, even to the end.

17   Pe

129 Your testimonies are wonderful; ◆
    therefore my soul keeps them.
130 The opening of your word gives light; ◆
    it gives understanding to the simple.
131 I open my mouth and draw in my breath, ◆
    as I long for your commandments.
132 Turn to me and be gracious to me, ◆
    as is your way with those who love your name.
133 Order my steps by your word, ◆
    and let no wickedness have dominion over me.
134 Redeem me from earthly oppressors ◆
    so that I may keep your commandments.
135 Show the light of your countenance upon your servant ◆
    and teach me your statutes.
136 My eyes run down with streams of water, ◆
    because the wicked do not keep your law.

18   Tsadhe

137 Righteous are you, O Lord, ◆
    and true are your judgements.
138 You have ordered your decrees in righteousness ◆
    and in great faithfulness.
139 My indignation destroys me, ◆
    because my adversaries forget your word.
140 Your word has been tried to the uttermost ◆
    and so your servant loves it.
141 I am small and of no reputation, ◆
    yet do I not forget your commandments.
142 Your righteousness is an everlasting righteousness ◆
    and your law is the truth.
143 Trouble and heaviness have taken hold upon me, ◆
    yet my delight is in your commandments.

144   The righteousness of your testimonies is everlasting; ◆
    O grant me understanding and I shall live.

Psalm 121

1   I lift up my eyes to the hills; ◆
    from where is my help to come?

2   My help comes from the Lord, ◆
    the maker of heaven and earth.

3   He will not suffer your foot to stumble; ◆
    he who watches over you will not sleep.

4   Behold, he who keeps watch over Israel ◆
    shall neither slumber nor sleep.

5   The Lord himself watches over you; ◆
    the Lord is your shade at your right hand,

6   So that the sun shall not strike you by day, ◆
    neither the moon by night.

7   The Lord shall keep you from all evil; ◆
    it is he who shall keep your soul.

8   The Lord shall keep watch over your going out
        and your coming in, ◆
    from this time forth for evermore.

Psalm 122

1   I was glad when they said to me, ◆
    'Let us go to the house of the Lord.'

2   And now our feet are standing ◆
    within your gates, O Jerusalem;

3   Jerusalem, built as a city ◆
    that is at unity in itself.

4   Thither the tribes go up, the tribes of the Lord, ◆
    as is decreed for Israel,
        to give thanks to the name of the Lord.

5   For there are set the thrones of judgement, ◆
    the thrones of the house of David.

6   O pray for the peace of Jerusalem: ◆
    'May they prosper who love you.

7   'Peace be within your walls ◆
    and tranquillity within your palaces.'

8   For my kindred and companions' sake, ◆
    I will pray that peace be with you.

9   For the sake of the house of the Lord our God, ◆
I will seek to do you good.

Psalm 123

1   To you I lift up my eyes, ◆
to you that are enthroned in the heavens.

2   As the eyes of servants look to the hand of their master, ◆
or the eyes of a maid to the hand of her mistress,

3   So our eyes wait upon the Lord our God, ◆
until he have mercy upon us.

4   Have mercy upon us, O Lord, have mercy upon us, ◆
for we have had more than enough of contempt.

5   Our soul has had more than enough of the scorn
of the arrogant, ◆
and of the contempt of the proud.

Psalm 124

1   If the Lord himself had not been on our side, ◆
now may Israel say;

2   If the Lord had not been on our side, ◆
when enemies rose up against us;

3   Then would they have swallowed us alive ◆
when their anger burned against us;

4   Then would the waters have overwhelmed us
and the torrent gone over our soul; ◆
over our soul would have swept the raging waters.

5   But blessed be the Lord ◆
who has not given us over to be a prey for their teeth.

6   Our soul has escaped
as a bird from the snare of the fowler; ◆
the snare is broken and we are delivered.

7   Our help is in the name of the Lord, ◆
who has made heaven and earth.

Psalm 125

1   Those who trust in the Lord are like Mount Zion, ◆
which cannot be moved, but stands fast for ever.

2   As the hills stand about Jerusalem, ◆
    so the Lord stands round about his people,
        from this time forth for evermore.
3   The sceptre of wickedness shall not hold sway
        over the land allotted to the righteous, ◆
    lest the righteous turn their hands to evil.
4   Do good, O Lord, to those who are good, ◆
    and to those who are true of heart.
5   Those who turn aside to crooked ways
        the Lord shall take away with the evildoers; ◆
    but let there be peace upon Israel.

Psalm 126

1   When the Lord restored the fortunes of Zion, ◆
    then were we like those who dream.
2   Then was our mouth filled with laughter ◆
    and our tongue with songs of joy.
3   Then said they among the nations, ◆
    'The Lord has done great things for them.'
4   The Lord has indeed done great things for us, ◆
    and therefore we rejoiced.
5   Restore again our fortunes, O Lord, ◆
    as the river beds of the desert.
6   Those who sow in tears ◆
    shall reap with songs of joy.
7   Those who go out weeping, bearing the seed, ◆
    will come back with shouts of joy,
        bearing their sheaves with them.

Psalm 127

1   Unless the Lord builds the house, ◆
    those who build it labour in vain.
2   Unless the Lord keeps the city, ◆
    the guard keeps watch in vain.
3   It is in vain that you hasten to rise up early
        and go so late to rest, eating the bread of toil, ◆
    for he gives his beloved sleep.

4   Children are a heritage from the Lord ✦
    and the fruit of the womb is his gift.
5   Like arrows in the hand of a warrior, ✦
    so are the children of one's youth.
6   Happy are those who have their quiver full of them: ✦
    they shall not be put to shame
        when they dispute with their enemies in the gate.

Psalm 128

1   Blessed are all those who fear the Lord, ✦
    and walk in his ways.
2   You shall eat the fruit of the toil of your hands; ✦
    it shall go well with you, and happy shall you be.
3   Your wife within your house
        shall be like a fruitful vine; ✦
    your children round your table,
        like fresh olive branches.
4   Thus shall the one be blest ✦
    who fears the Lord.
5   The Lord from out of Zion bless you, ✦
    that you may see Jerusalem in prosperity
        all the days of your life.
6   May you see your children's children, ✦
    and may there be peace upon Israel.

Psalm 130

1   Out of the depths have I cried to you, O Lord;
        Lord, hear my voice; ✦
    let your ears consider well the voice of my supplication.
2   If you, Lord, were to mark what is done amiss, ✦
    O Lord, who could stand?
3   But there is forgiveness with you, ✦
    so that you shall be feared.
4   I wait for the Lord; my soul waits for him; ✦
    in his word is my hope.
5   My soul waits for the Lord,
        more than the night watch for the morning, ✦
    more than the night watch for the morning.

6   O Israel, wait for the Lord, ♦
for with the Lord there is mercy;

7   With him is plenteous redemption ♦
and he shall redeem Israel from all their sins.

Psalm 131

1   O Lord, my heart is not proud; ♦
my eyes are not raised in haughty looks.

2   I do not occupy myself with great matters, ♦
with things that are too high for me.

3   But I have quieted and stilled my soul,
like a weaned child on its mother's breast; ♦
so my soul is quieted within me.

4   O Israel, trust in the Lord, ♦
from this time forth for evermore.

Psalm 132

1   Lord, remember for David ♦
all the hardships he endured;

2   How he swore an oath to the Lord ♦
and vowed a vow to the Mighty One of Jacob:

3   'I will not come within the shelter of my house, ♦
nor climb up into my bed;

4   'I will not allow my eyes to sleep, ♦
nor let my eyelids slumber,

5   'Until I find a place for the Lord, ♦
a dwelling for the Mighty One of Jacob.'

6   Now, we heard of the ark in Ephrathah ♦
and found it in the fields of Ja-ar.

7   Let us enter his dwelling place ♦
and fall low before his footstool.

8   Arise, O Lord, into your resting place, ♦
you and the ark of your strength.

9   Let your priests be clothed with righteousness ♦
and your faithful ones sing with joy.

10   For your servant David's sake, ♦
turn not away the face of your anointed.

11 The Lord has sworn an oath to David, ♦
    a promise from which he will not shrink:
12 'Of the fruit of your body ♦
    shall I set upon your throne.
13 'If your children keep my covenant
        and my testimonies that I shall teach them, ♦
    their children also shall sit upon your throne for evermore.'
14 For the Lord has chosen Zion for himself; ♦
    he has desired her for his habitation:
15 'This shall be my resting place for ever; ♦
    here will I dwell, for I have longed for her.
16 'I will abundantly bless her provision; ♦
    her poor will I satisfy with bread.
17 'I will clothe her priests with salvation, ♦
    and her faithful ones shall rejoice and sing.
18 'There will I make a horn to spring up for David; ♦
    I will keep a lantern burning for my anointed.
19 'As for his enemies, I will clothe them with shame; ♦
    but on him shall his crown be bright.'

Psalm 133

1   Behold how good and pleasant it is ♦
    to dwell together in unity.
2   It is like the precious oil upon the head, ♦
    running down upon the beard,
3   Even on Aaron's beard, ♦
    running down upon the collar of his clothing.
4   It is like the dew of Hermon ♦
    running down upon the hills of Zion.
5   For there the Lord has promised his blessing: ♦
    even life for evermore.

Psalm 136

1   Give thanks to the Lord, for he is gracious, ♦
    for his mercy endures for ever.
2   Give thanks to the God of gods, ♦
    for his mercy endures for ever.

3   Give thanks to the Lord of lords, ◆
       for his mercy endures for ever;

4   Who alone does great wonders, ◆
       for his mercy endures for ever;

5   Who by wisdom made the heavens, ◆
       for his mercy endures for ever;

6   Who laid out the earth upon the waters, ◆
       for his mercy endures for ever;

7   Who made the great lights, ◆
       for his mercy endures for ever;

8   The sun to rule the day, ◆
       for his mercy endures for ever;

9   The moon and the stars to govern the night, ◆
       for his mercy endures for ever;

10   Who smote the firstborn of Egypt, ◆
       for his mercy endures for ever;

11   And brought out Israel from among them, ◆
       for his mercy endures for ever;

12   With a mighty hand and outstretched arm, ◆
       for his mercy endures for ever;

13   Who divided the Red Sea in two, ◆
       for his mercy endures for ever;

14   And made Israel to pass through the midst of it, ◆
       for his mercy endures for ever;

15   But Pharaoh and his host he overthrew in the Red Sea, ◆
       for his mercy endures for ever;

16   Who led his people through the wilderness, ◆
       for his mercy endures for ever;

17   Who smote great kings, ◆
       for his mercy endures for ever;

18   And slew mighty kings, ◆
       for his mercy endures for ever;

19   Sihon, king of the Amorites, ◆
       for his mercy endures for ever;

20   And Og, the king of Bashan, ◆
       for his mercy endures for ever;

21   And gave away their land for a heritage, ◆
       for his mercy endures for ever;

22 A heritage for Israel his servant, ◆
    for his mercy endures for ever;

23 Who remembered us when we were in trouble, ◆
    for his mercy endures for ever;
24 And delivered us from our enemies, ◆
    for his mercy endures for ever;
25 Who gives food to all creatures, ◆
    for his mercy endures for ever.
26 Give thanks to the God of heaven, ◆
    for his mercy endures for ever.

Psalm 137

1   By the waters of Babylon we sat down and wept, ◆
    when we remembered Zion.
2   As for our lyres, we hung them up ◆
    on the willows that grow in that land.
3   For there our captors asked for a song,
        our tormentors called for mirth: ◆
    'Sing us one of the songs of Zion.'
4   How shall we sing the Lord's song ◆
    in a strange land?
5   If I forget you, O Jerusalem, ◆
    let my right hand forget its skill.
6   Let my tongue cleave to the roof of my mouth
        if I do not remember you, ◆
    if I set not Jerusalem above my highest joy.

7   Remember, O Lord, against the people of Edom
        the day of Jerusalem, ◆
    how they said, 'Down with it, down with it,
        even to the ground.'
8   O daughter of Babylon, doomed to destruction, ◆
    happy the one who repays you
        for all you have done to us;
9   Who takes your little ones, ◆
    and dashes them against the rock.

1 I will give thanks to you, O Lord, with my whole heart; ◆
before the gods will I sing praise to you.

2 I will bow down towards your holy temple
and praise your name,
because of your love and faithfulness; ◆
for you have glorified your name
and your word above all things.

3 In the day that I called to you, you answered me; ◆
you put new strength in my soul.

4 All the kings of the earth shall praise you, O Lord, ◆
for they have heard the words of your mouth.

5 They shall sing of the ways of the Lord, ◆
that great is the glory of the Lord.

6 Though the Lord be high, he watches over the lowly; ◆
as for the proud, he regards them from afar.

7 Though I walk in the midst of trouble,
you will preserve me; ◆
you will stretch forth your hand against the fury of my enemies;
your right hand will save me.

8 The Lord shall make good his purpose for me; ◆
your loving-kindness, O Lord, endures for ever;
forsake not the work of your hands.

1 O Lord, you have searched me out and known me; ◆
you know my sitting down and my rising up;
you discern my thoughts from afar.

2 You mark out my journeys and my resting place ◆
and are acquainted with all my ways.

3 For there is not a word on my tongue, ◆
but you, O Lord, know it altogether.

4 You encompass me behind and before ◆
and lay your hand upon me.

5 Such knowledge is too wonderful for me, ◆
so high that I cannot attain it.

12   For you yourself created my inmost parts; ♦
you knit me together in my mother's womb.

13   I thank you, for I am fearfully and wonderfully made; ♦
marvellous are your works, my soul knows well.

14   My frame was not hidden from you, ♦
when I was made in secret
    and woven in the depths of the earth.

15   Your eyes beheld my form, as yet unfinished; ♦
already in your book were all my members written,

16   As day by day they were fashioned ♦
when as yet there was none of them.

17   How deep are your counsels to me, O God! ♦
How great is the sum of them!

23   Search me out, O God, and know my heart; ♦
try me and examine my thoughts.

24   See if there is any way of wickedness in me ♦
and lead me in the way everlasting.

Psalm 145

1   I will exalt you, O God my King, ♦
and bless your name for ever and ever.

2   Every day will I bless you ♦
and praise your name for ever and ever.

3   Great is the Lord and highly to be praised; ♦
his greatness is beyond all searching out.

4   One generation shall praise your works to another ♦
and declare your mighty acts.

5   They shall speak of the majesty of your glory, ♦
and I will tell of all your wonderful deeds.

6   They shall speak of the might of your marvellous acts, ♦
and I will also tell of your greatness.

7   They shall pour forth the story of your abundant kindness ♦
and joyfully sing of your righteousness.

8   The Lord is gracious and merciful, ♦
long-suffering and of great goodness.

9   The Lord is loving to everyone ♦
and his mercy is over all his creatures.

10   All your works praise you, O Lord, ♦
      and your faithful servants bless you.

11   They tell of the glory of your kingdom ♦
      and speak of your mighty power,

12   To make known to all peoples your mighty acts ♦
      and the glorious splendour of your kingdom.

13   Your kingdom is an everlasting kingdom; ♦
      your dominion endures throughout all ages.

14   The Lord is sure in all his words ♦
      and faithful in all his deeds.

15   The Lord upholds all those who fall ♦
      and lifts up all those who are bowed down.

16   The eyes of all wait upon you, O Lord, ♦
      and you give them their food in due season.

17   You open wide your hand ♦
      and fill all things living with plenty.

18   The Lord is righteous in all his ways ♦
      and loving in all his works.

19   The Lord is near to those who call upon him, ♦
      to all who call upon him faithfully.

20   He fulfils the desire of those who fear him; ♦
      he hears their cry and saves them.

21   The Lord watches over those who love him, ♦
      but all the wicked shall he destroy.

22   My mouth shall speak the praise of the Lord, ♦
      and let all flesh bless his holy name for ever and ever.

Psalm 146

1   Alleluia.
      Praise the Lord, O my soul:
      while I live will I praise the Lord; ♦
    as long as I have any being,
      I will sing praises to my God.

2   Put not your trust in princes,
      nor in any human power, ♦
    for there is no help in them.

3   When their breath goes forth, they return to the earth; ♦
      on that day all their thoughts perish.

4   Happy are those who have the God of Jacob for their help, ◆
     whose hope is in the Lord their God;
5   Who made heaven and earth,
         the sea and all that is in them; ◆
     who keeps his promise for ever;
6   Who gives justice to those that suffer wrong ◆
     and bread to those who hunger.
7   The Lord looses those that are bound; ◆
     the Lord opens the eyes of the blind;
8   The Lord lifts up those who are bowed down; ◆
     the Lord loves the righteous;
9   The Lord watches over the stranger in the land;
         he upholds the orphan and widow; ◆
     but the way of the wicked he turns upside down.
10   The Lord shall reign for ever, ◆
     your God, O Zion, throughout all generations.
         Alleluia.

Psalm 147

1   Alleluia.
         How good it is to make music for our God, ◆
     how joyful to honour him with praise.
2   The Lord builds up Jerusalem ◆
     and gathers together the outcasts of Israel.
3   He heals the brokenhearted ◆
     and binds up all their wounds.
4   He counts the number of the stars ◆
     and calls them all by their names.
5   Great is our Lord and mighty in power; ◆
     his wisdom is beyond all telling.
6   The Lord lifts up the poor, ◆
     but casts down the wicked to the ground.
7   Sing to the Lord with thanksgiving; ◆
     make music to our God upon the lyre;
8   Who covers the heavens with clouds ◆
     and prepares rain for the earth;
9   Who makes grass to grow upon the mountains ◆
     and green plants to serve our needs.

10	He gives the beasts their food ◆
	and the young ravens when they cry.
11	He takes no pleasure in the power of a horse, ◆
	no delight in human strength;
12	But the Lord delights in those who fear him, ◆
	who put their trust in his steadfast love.

13	Sing praise to the Lord, O Jerusalem; ◆
	praise your God, O Zion;
14	For he has strengthened the bars of your gates ◆
	and has blest your children within you.
15	He has established peace in your borders ◆
	and satisfies you with the finest wheat.
16	He sends forth his command to the earth ◆
	and his word runs very swiftly.
17	He gives snow like wool ◆
	and scatters the hoarfrost like ashes.
18	He casts down his hailstones like morsels of bread; ◆
	who can endure his frost?
19	He sends forth his word and melts them; ◆
	he blows with his wind and the waters flow.
20	He declares his word to Jacob, ◆
	his statutes and judgements to Israel.
21	He has not dealt so with any other nation; ◆
	they do not know his laws.
	Alleluia.

Psalm 148

1	Alleluia.
	Praise the Lord from the heavens; ◆
	praise him in the heights.
2	Praise him, all you his angels; ◆
	praise him, all his host.
3	Praise him, sun and moon; ◆
	praise him, all you stars of light.
4	Praise him, heaven of heavens, ◆
	and you waters above the heavens.
5	Let them praise the name of the Lord, ◆
	for he commanded and they were created.

6   He made them fast for ever and ever; ♦
he gave them a law which shall not pass away.

7   Praise the Lord from the earth, ♦
you sea monsters and all deeps;
8   Fire and hail, snow and mist, ♦
tempestuous wind, fulfilling his word;
9   Mountains and all hills, ♦
fruit trees and all cedars;
10   Wild beasts and all cattle, ♦
creeping things and birds on the wing;
11   Kings of the earth and all peoples, ♦
princes and all rulers of the world;
12   Young men and women,
old and young together; ♦
let them praise the name of the Lord.
13   For his name only is exalted, ♦
his splendour above earth and heaven.
14   He has raised up the horn of his people
and praise for all his faithful servants, ♦
the children of Israel, a people who are near him.
Alleluia.

Psalm 149

1   Alleluia.
O sing to the Lord a new song; ♦
sing his praise in the congregation of the faithful.
2   Let Israel rejoice in their maker; ♦
let the children of Zion be joyful in their king.
3   Let them praise his name in the dance; ♦
let them sing praise to him with timbrel and lyre.
4   For the Lord has pleasure in his people ♦
and adorns the poor with salvation.
5   Let the faithful be joyful in glory; ♦
let them rejoice in their ranks,
6   With the praises of God in their mouths ♦
and a two-edged sword in their hands;
7   To execute vengeance on the nations ♦
and punishment on the peoples;

8   To bind their kings in chains ◆
    and their nobles with fetters of iron;
9   To execute on them the judgement decreed: ◆
    such honour have all his faithful servants.
        Alleluia.

Psalm 150

1   Alleluia.
        O praise God in his holiness; ◆
    praise him in the firmament of his power.
2   Praise him for his mighty acts; ◆
    praise him according to his excellent greatness.
3   Praise him with the blast of the trumpet; ◆
    praise him upon the harp and lyre.
4   Praise him with timbrel and dances; ◆
    praise him upon the strings and pipe.
5   Praise him with ringing cymbals; ◆
    praise him upon the clashing cymbals.
6   Let everything that has breath ◆
    praise the Lord.
        Alleluia.

Canticles

Benedictus (The Song of Zechariah)

1   Blessed be the Lord the God of Israel, ◆
    who has come to his people and set them free.
2   He has raised up for us a mighty Saviour, ◆
    born of the house of his servant David.
3   Through his holy prophets God promised of old ◆
    to save us from our enemies,
        from the hands of all that hate us,
4   To show mercy to our ancestors, ◆
    and to remember his holy covenant.
5   This was the oath God swore to our father Abraham: ◆
    to set us free from the hands of our enemies,

6 Free to worship him without fear, ♦
   holy and righteous in his sight
      all the days of our life.
7 And you, child, shall be called the prophet of the Most High, ♦
   for you will go before the Lord to prepare his way,
8 To give his people knowledge of salvation ♦
   by the forgiveness of all their sins.
9 In the tender compassion of our God ♦
   the dawn from on high shall break upon us,
10 To shine on those who dwell in darkness
      and the shadow of death, ♦
   and to guide our feet into the way of peace. (Luke 1.68–79)

   Glory to the Father and to the Son
   and to the Holy Spirit;
   as it was in the beginning is now
   and shall be for ever. Amen.

A Song of Deliverance

1 'Behold, God is my salvation; ♦
   I will trust and will not be afraid;
2 'For the Lord God is my strength and my song, ♦
   and has become my salvation.'
3 With joy you will draw water ♦
   from the wells of salvation.
4 On that day you will say, ♦
   'Give thanks to the Lord, call upon his name;
5 'Make known his deeds among the nations, ♦
   proclaim that his name is exalted.
6 'Sing God's praises, who has triumphed gloriously; ♦
   let this be known in all the world.
7 'Shout and sing for joy, you that dwell in Zion, ♦
   for great in your midst is the Holy One of Israel.' (Isaiah 12.2–6)

   Glory to the Father and to the Son
   and to the Holy Spirit;
   as it was in the beginning is now
   and shall be for ever. Amen.

Magnificat (The Song of Mary)

1   My soul proclaims the greatness of the Lord,
        my spirit rejoices in God my Saviour; ◆
    he has looked with favour on his lowly servant.

2   From this day all generations will call me blessed; ◆
    the Almighty has done great things for me
        and holy is his name.

3   He has mercy on those who fear him, ◆
    from generation to generation.

4   He has shown strength with his arm ◆
    and has scattered the proud in their conceit,

5   Casting down the mighty from their thrones ◆
    and lifting up the lowly.

6   He has filled the hungry with good things ◆
    and sent the rich away empty.

7   He has come to the aid of his servant Israel, ◆
    to remember his promise of mercy,

8   The promise made to our ancestors, ◆
    to Abraham and his children for ever. (Luke 1.46–55)

Glory to the Father and to the Son
and to the Holy Spirit;
as it was in the beginning is now
and shall be for ever. Amen.

PRAYERS FOR DAILY LIFE AND OCCASIONS AT HOME

Lord Jesus Christ,
alive and at large in the world,
help me to follow and find you there today
in the places where I work,
   meet people,
   spend money
   and make plans.
Take me as a disciple of your kingdom,
to see through your eyes
   and hear the questions you are asking,
to welcome all with your trust and truth
   and to change the things that contradict God's love
by the power of the cross
   and the freedom of your Spirit.
Amen.   (John V. Taylor)

Thanks be to thee, O Lord Christ,
for all the benefits that thou hast given us,
for all the pains and insults which thou hast borne for us.
O most merciful redeemer, friend and brother,
may I know thee more clearly,
love thee more dearly
and follow thee more nearly,
day by day.
Amen.   (Richard of Chichester)

O Lord, support us all the day long of this troublous life,
until the shadows lengthen and the evening comes,
the busy world is hushed,
the fever of life is over,
and our work is done.
Then, Lord, in your mercy,
grant us safe lodging,
a holy rest, and peace at the last.
Amen.   (John Henry Newman)

World prayer for peace

O God, lead us from death to life,
from falsehood to truth.
Lead us from despair to hope,
from fear to trust.
Lead us from hate to love,
from war to peace.
Let peace fill our hearts, our world, our universe.
Amen.   (Satish Kumar; adapted)

Dearest Lord, teach me to be generous,
teach me to serve thee as thou deservest,
to give and not to count the cost,
to fight and not to heed the wounds,
to toil and not to seek for rest,
to labour and not to seek reward,
save that of knowing that I do thy will.
Amen.   (Ignatius Loyola)

Approaching death

God be in my head,
and in my understanding;
God be in mine eyes,
and in my looking;
God be in my mouth,
and in my speaking;
God be in my heart,
and in my thinking;
God be at mine end,
and at my departing.   (*Sarum Primer*)